LIME

Quarrying and Limemaking in the San Juan Islands

Boyd C. Pratt

Mulno Cove Publishing
FRIDAY HARBOR

Lime (CaO) [*lahym*]:
A white or grayish-white, odorless, lumpy solid produced from heating limestone.

Lime:
Quarrying and Limemaking in the San Juan Islands

by Boyd C. Pratt

Copyright © 2022 Boyd C. Pratt
All rights reserved

Second Edition

No part of this publication may be reproduced or transmitted in English or in other languages, in any form or by any means, electronic or mechanical, including photocopying, digital scanning, recording, or any other informational storage or retrieval system, without the written permission of the author.

ISBN: 978-1-7342351-3-5

Published by Mulno Cove Publishing
Printed in the United States of America

Table of Contents

Origins 1
Early Operations 3
Small Time Production 11
Economics of the Lime Industry 12
Uses of Lime..13
Making Lime 15
Dangerous Cargo 18
Life at the Lime Kilns...20
Cowell v. McMillin..22
Competition and Controversy..24
Portland Cement 27
Depression and Decline 29
Legacy 31

Tour Guides: Limekiln Sites in San Juan County
Lime Kiln...33
Roche Harbor...41
Judd Cove 51

Suggested Reading 54
Illustration Credits 56
Acknowledgements 57
Firebricks Used in San Juan Islands Lime Kilns................59
Lime Companies in the San Juan Islands 61
Limemakers in the San Juan Islands.................................71

LIMESTONE QUARRIES AND LIME KILNS IN SAN JUAN COUNTY

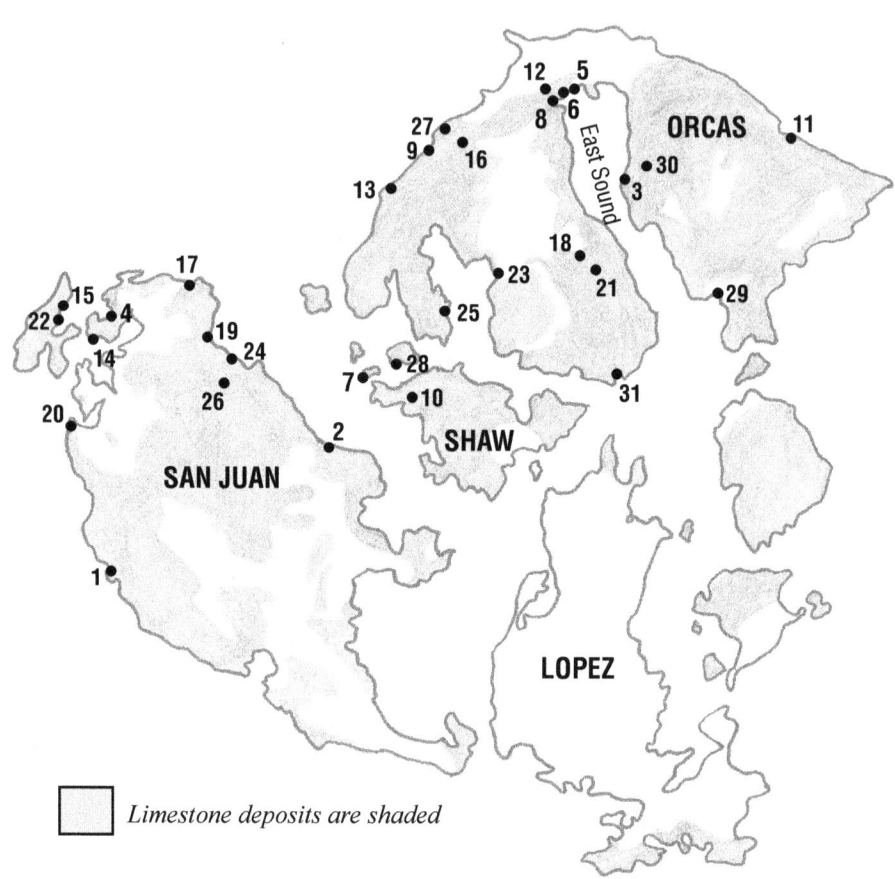

1. **San Juan Lime Company** 1860-1888; Cowell's 1888-1957 (*see tour guide p.33*)
2. **Eureka** Roberts 1861?; McLachlan Brothers 1870s; Thomas Lee and Robert Caines 1880s; Werner 1890s
3. **Port Langdon** George Shotter 1862; McLachlan Brothers 1874
4. **Roche Harbor** Scurr Brothers 1879-1886; Tacoma and Roche Harbor Lime Company 1886-1905; Roche Harbor Lime & Cement Co. 1905-1956 (*see tour guide p.41*)
5. **Gailey and Boyd** pre-1888
6. **Bowen Brothers & Jamieson** pre-1888
7. **Cliff Island** Tift 1888-1894; Everett Smelter Company 1895; Manufacturer's Mineral Mining Co.1947
8. **Gregg's** McCurdy Lime Company 1888; Gregg's 1889 (*see tour guide p.51*)
9. **Eagle Lime Company** Lee Wheeler 1889; Eagle Lime Company 1900; Orcas Lime Company 1904.
10. **Lutz Quarry** Tift 1890s: Everett Smelter Company up to 1895
11. **Estelle** 1894; Chuckanut Limestone Company 1906
12. **Double Hill** 1890s?
13. **Island Lime Company** Imperial Lime Co. 1900; Cowell Lime Co. 1904
14. **White Point** Orcas Lime Company 1923
15. **Henry Island 1** Roche Harbor Lime & Cement Co. pre-1925
16. **Soderberg** Soderberg pre-1927; Cowell's; Everett Lime Co. 1958
17. **Limestone Point** Roche Harbor Lime & Cement Co. pre-1927
18. **McGraw-Kittinger** Westerman Lime & Rock pre-1927; Everett Lime Company
19. **Rocky Bay** Pulp mill quarrying ca. 1929
20. **Mitchell Bay** Puget Sound Pulp & Timber Co. 1933
21. **Pineo** Soundview Company (Everett) 1934-36
22. **Henry Island 2**, Dr. J. J. Schultz, limestone sold to Orcas Lime Company pre-1936
23. **West Sound** Roche Harbor Lime & Cement Co. ca. 1936; Everett Lime Company 1957
24. **Wilson** Everett Lime Company pre-1941
25. **Krumdick** pre-1941
26. **Johnson** Mitchell Bay Lime Co. pre-1941
27. **Red Cross** Roche Harbor Lime & Cement Co. pre-1943; Everett Lime Co. 1940s
28. **Crane Island** date unknown
29. **Newhall** 1908-1909
30. **Payton** (Flaherty) date unknown
31. **Grindstone Harbor** date unknown

Lime:
Quarrying and Limemaking in the San Juan Islands

East Sound Lime Kiln and Dock, Orcas Island, 1888

For more than 60 years—from 1860 until the 1920s—San Juan County was the principal lime-producing area in the state of Washington. The San Juan Islands were ideal for the manufacture and transport of lime. Large deposits of high-quality limestone were located right on the shoreline with good deep-water harbors, protected from prevailing winds. Operating largely by gravity, the quarried limestone was shunted downhill to the top of the kilns, fired with high-temperature-producing old growth Douglas fir, and then drawn out from the bottom of the kilns as lime. Packed in barrels, the final product was transferred to warehouses built on or close to wharves. Fleets of ships, both sail and steam, regularly transported the lime to Puget Sound, West Coast, and Pacific Rim markets where it was in demand as a building-construction material and as an important ingredient for several growing regional industries, including smelting and papermaking.

ORIGINS

Calcium (Ca), the fifth most abundant element on earth, is a silvery-white metal, occurring naturally in chalk, gypsum, and limestone. **Limestone** is a sedimentary rock composed mostly of the minerals calcite and aragonite, which are crystal forms of **calcium carbonate** ($CaCO_3$). **Marble** is limestone altered by heat, pressure, or other natural agency (metamorphism). **Lime** (CaO) is a white, odorless solid that is produced by heating calcium carbonate in the form of limestone or sea shells. Lime combined with water forms **calcium hydroxide** ($Ca(OH)_2$) also known as slaked lime.

Lime is produced from limestone, a sedimentary rock consisting primarily of calcium carbonate metamorphosed into aragonite in the form of marble. Limestone deposits in the San Juan Islands extend from the northeastern portion of Orcas, across the island to the northern and western portions of San Juan, and include the smaller islands in between such as Crane, Jones, and Shaw. The geology of the San Juans is extremely complex, but local limestone is predominately from two terranes. (A terrane is a discrete fault-bounded layer of rock that typically formed in one location and was transported by tectonic movement to another.) The older Turtleback/Eastsound Terrane dates from the 415-to-260 million years ago; it is found on the west coast of Orcas. The Deadman Bay/Orcas Terrane, from 280-190 million years ago, the primary source of limestone in the San Juan Islands, is found at Lime Kiln, Roche Harbor, and other locations on northern San Juan Island and throughout much of Orcas

> *The limestones of western Washington were originally formed as horizontal or nearly horizontal layers, mounds, and lenses on the sea floor. They have since been lifted above the sea and tilted, complexly folded, squeezed into irregular shapes, and broken by faulting.*
>
> —Wilbert R. Danner,
> *Limestone Resources of Western Washington*

Island. Both consist of basalt inter-fingered by thin beds, or lenses, of limestone, which is what is quarried. Their formation is like the atoll island system of the tropical Pacific, where lava erupts, cools in the ocean, and is subsequently covered by limey mud—calcium that was dissolved in seawater combined with carbon dioxide to form the solid calcite—and reefs formed from organisms that absorbed calcium to form shells and skeletons and then died. Neither terrane, though, formed near its present location: eastward movement of the Farallon Plate under the Pacific Ocean carried the basalts and limestones of the Deadman Bay/Orcas Terrane and accreted, or attached, them to the North American Plate over 100 million years ago. (Evidence of their age and origin comes from single-celled invertebrate fossils in the limestones, known as fusulinids, which formed in the Tethys Sea near ancestral southeast China.) In contrast, geochemical analysis of the Turtleback/Eastsound Terrane suggests that it formed as an island volcanic arc initially near the North Atlantic. It subsequently migrated along the northern edge of the continent of North America where limestone reefs developed along its ancient volcanos before it was accreted to the West Coast.

North Kiln and Boarding House, Lime Kiln, San Juan Island

EARLY OPERATIONS

> *The value of these discoveries can better be appreciated from the fact that up to the time of the discovery of limestone on this island it was not known to exist at any point on Puget Sound, within United States territory, and for building purposes it was necessary to procure all the lime used, from California or Vancouver's Island.*
>
> –Geographical Memoir, U. S. North West Boundary Survey

The U. S. North West Boundary Survey first discovered and tested limestone on the west and north side of San Juan Island in 1859. Quarrying and processing began on San Juan at Roche Harbor when the Royal Marines established an encampment at the north end of the island (English Camp) as part of the agreement between the United States of America and Great Britain to jointly occupy San Juan Island until the resolution of the Pig War territorial question. They used the lime for paint, whitewash, and mortar in the construction of their buildings.

The first commercial operation began in 1860, when Lyman Cutlar, whose shooting of a Hudson's Bay Company pig had touched off the Pig War controversy, partnered with E. C. Gillette and Frank Newsome to produce lime on the west side of San Juan. Gillette sold his interest to Augustin Hibbard after the first winter of operation, and the three formed a new business—the San Juan Lime Company.

Eureka, located just north of Friday Harbor on the east coast of San Juan, was founded in the

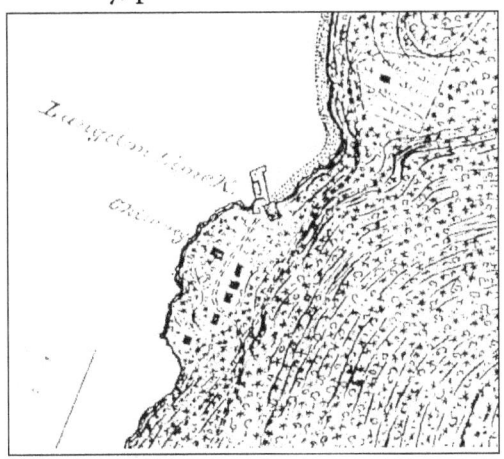

Langdon Lime Kiln, Orcas Island, 1889

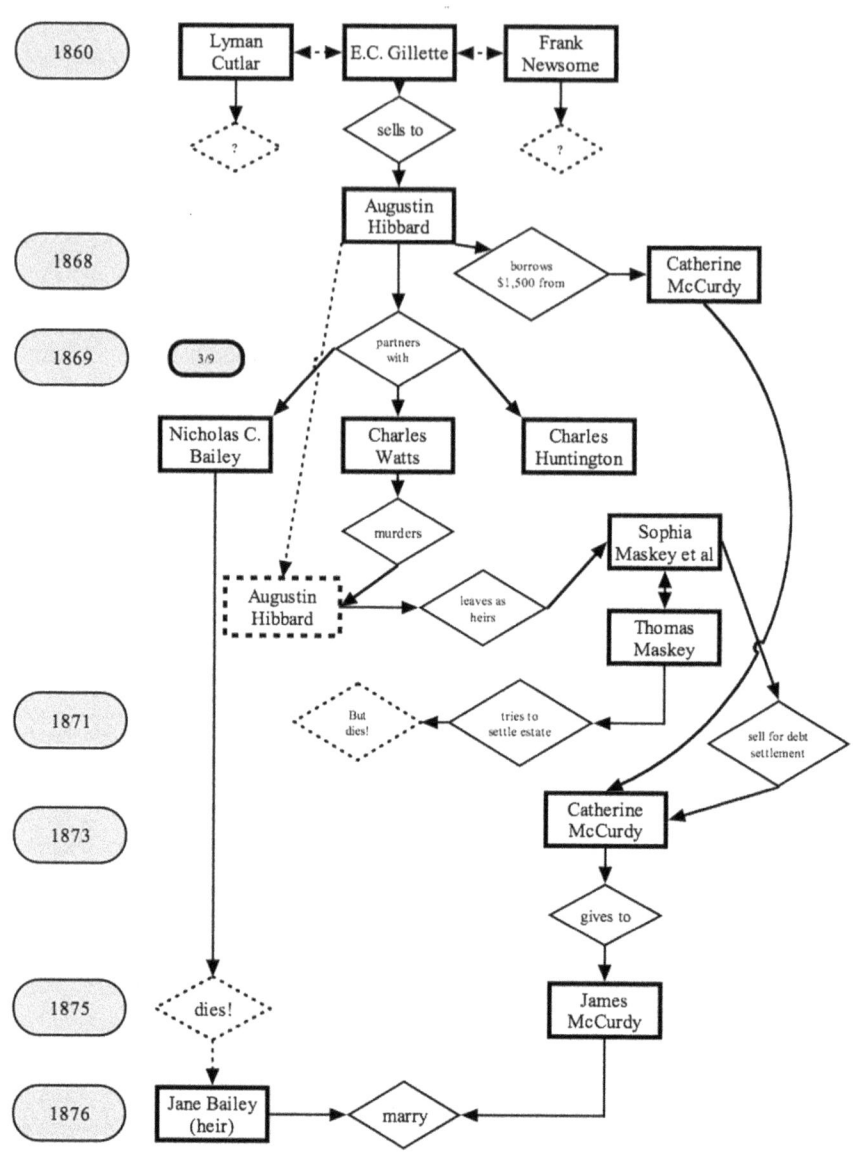

San Juan Lime Company, Chart of Ownership, 1860-1876

early 1860s by an Englishman named Roberts; it was later owned and operated by Daniel and William McLachlan and their cousin by marriage, Thomas Lee. Port Langdon, on the east shore of Orcas Island's East Sound, was first quarried in 1862 by George R. Shotter.

The said Charles Watts on the seventeenth day of June A. D. 1869 in the county of Whatcom...in and upon one Augustin Hibbard purposely and of deliberate and premeditated malice did make an assault and that the said Charles Watts, a certain pistol, then and there charged with gunpower and two leaden bullets then and there purposely and of deliberate and premeditated malice did discharge, and shoot off, to, against, and upon, the said Augustin Hibbard, and that the said Charles Watts, with leaden bullets aforesaid, out of the pistol aforesaid, then and there by the force of the gunpowder aforesaid, by the said Charles Watts discharged and shot off, as aforesaid, then and there purposely and of deliberate and premeditated malice, did then and there strike, penetrate, and wound, the said Augustin Hibbard, giving to him the said Augustin Hibbard then and there with the leaden bullets aforesaid, so as aforesaid discharged and shot out of the pistol aforesaid, by the said Charles Watts in and upon the face and breast of the said Augustin Hibbard, two mortal wounds each, of the depth of three inches, and of the width of one half inch, of which said mortal wounds, the said Augustin Hibbard then and there immediately died.
—Territory of Washington v. Charles Watts
Third Judicial District of Washington Territory, Port Townsend
14th September 1871

Hibbard bought out Cutlar and Newsome at the end of 1864, and continued operations until the following year, when George R. Shotter and Company bought in. In 1868 Hibbard borrowed $1,500 for operations from Catherine McCurdy of Port Townsend, secured through a mortgage on the land, and bought out Shotter. A year later, he formed a partnership with Nicholas C. Bailey, Charles Huntington, and Charles Watts. This agreement was shattered three months later, when Watts murdered Hibbard. Court-appointed appraisers prepared inventories of the property, and the heirs petitioned for distribution of the estate in 1871. The court eventually ordered the sale of the property to cover numerous debts and the mortgage with Catherine McCurdy. The property was sold in 1873 to none other than Catherine McCurdy for $1,500, thus both paying off her own mortgage and obtaining full title to the land and improvements in the process. She turned it over to her son, James, to operate with former San Juan Lime Company partner N. C. Bailey.

THE LIME KILN

. . . is situated on a side hill composed of solid, gray and brown stone. The rock which is manufactured into lime is contained in a ledge about 150 feet across and extending several hundred yards back; the quarry where great pieces of stone are blown off and broken up with blasting powder being in front. The kiln is a square pyramid constructed of massive stone masonry; is about 18 feet across each side at the base; is something over 20 feet high, and contains a vertical cavity about six feet in diameter. In this a fire is kept going constantly, consuming about 4 cords every 24 hours. The quarry is about 80 feet above the salt water; and the kiln, being situated below it, receives the fine broken pieces of rock at its top through a shute. Here are turned out, labeled ready for market, about 70 barrels per day of the finest quality of lime in the world. From 15 to 20 men are kept in employment to carry on the business; and the expenses are estimated at nearly $1200 per month. For pluck, experience, and genuine business capacity, Mr. McCurdy takes rank among the foremost men in our country, and if there were only more of the same kind the resources of Puget Sound would soon be developed to an extent worthy of their value. With his aid and that of his pleasant foreman, Mr. Scurr, we were enabled to "do up" the enterprise in a short time. The process of making the barrels we witnessed with no little interest. Several coopers are employed. Strong, light, durable barrels are made from cedar staves and young fir hoops. These are taken to a shed just below the kiln, where they are filled, headed up, and sent down on an ingeniously-constructed double railway track to the warehouse which is situated just above the wharf, and which will hold about 1,500 barrels. Here the proprietor showed us what he called "an affecting sight"– a great many barrels in tiers; whereupon we remarked that it was a kind of paradox, since they were so dry. Mr. McCurdy also keeps a store in the lower part of the building occupied by himself and family.

Editorial Correspondence from San Juan Island
Puget Sound Argus May 18, 1877

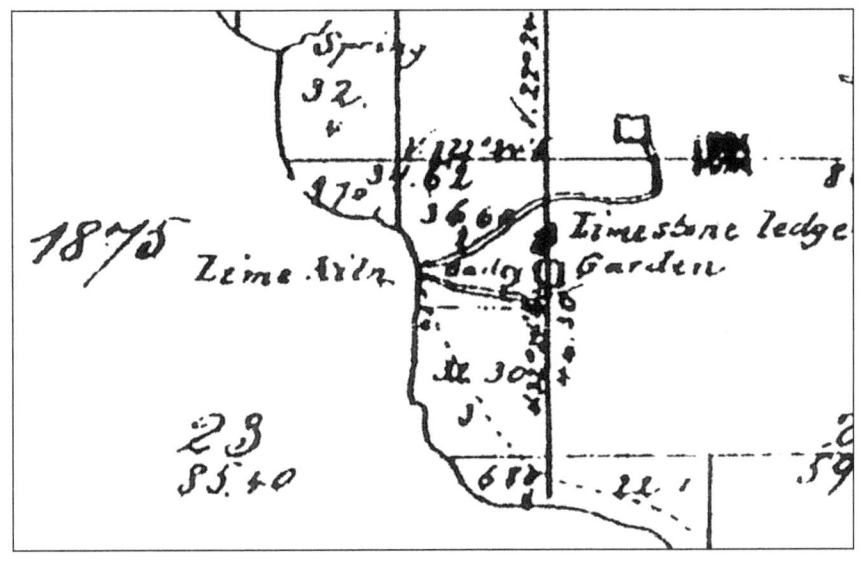

Bailey's Lime Kiln, Township and Range Survey, 1875

The two men soon secured a contract to supply lime for the new territorial prison at Steilacoom in Puget Sound. Within a few years, they had expanded production to 20,000 barrels per year. Then Bailey died, leaving his half of the company and property to his wife, Jane, and their two children. Within a few years, Jane married James McCurdy, thus uniting their ownership of the operations, then referred to as "McCurdy's."

The Timber and Stone Act of 1878

In addition to preemption and homestead claims, limestone deposits could be obtained through the Timber and Stone Act of 1878, which allowed private individuals to purchase 160 acres of land "unfit for farming" for $2.50 per acre. The purpose of the act was to develop timber and mining claims, and in San Juan County there were several limestone claims made, including James McCurdy at Lime Kiln on the west side of San Juan Island at the San Juan Lime Company and Alpheus Byers at the Island Lime Company on the west coast of Orcas Island.

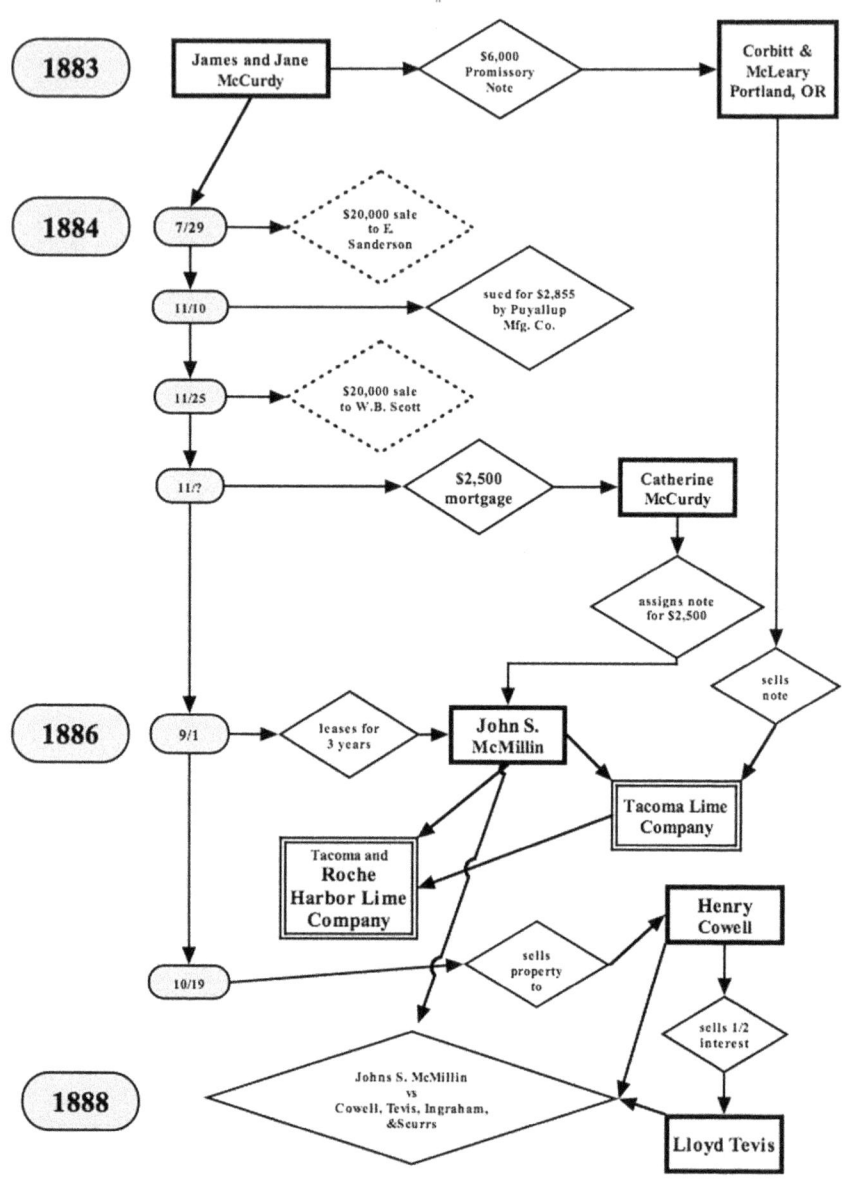

San Juan Lime Company, Chart of Ownership, 1883 -1888

In 1879, Richard and Robert Scurr bought property at Roche Harbor and, in conjunction with brothers Alexander and Donald Ross and their cousin Colin, developed two kilns. John S. McMillin bought the property and works in 1886 from the Scurrs and Rosses, establishing the Tacoma and Roche Harbor Lime Company. During the early 1880s, McCurdy's operation (San Juan Lime Company) began to slip, and production dropped to 7,000 barrels per year. Perhaps in desperation, McCurdy began borrowing heavily from several sources. McCurdy's mother sold her promissory note and mortgage to McMillin, who then leased the property from James and Jane McCurdy for three years, beginning in September 1886. One month later, the McCurdys sold their property to Henry Cowell of San Francisco, who in turn sold a half interest to his California partner Lloyd Tevis. Cowell refused to pay the mortgages on the property, forcing foreclosure by the Tacoma and Roche Harbor Lime Company; he then picked up the property at the subsequent sheriff's sale. McMillin responded by filing suit against Cowell, Tevis, Lee Ingram, and Richard and Robert Scurr—the latter three hired to work the quarries at that time—claiming that they were depleting the resources on land leased to McMillin. In this, the first of several legal battles between McMillin and Cowell, the judge eventually found for the defendants and dismissed the case.

Roche Harbor during the Scurr era

Langdon Lime Kiln and Dock, Orcas Island, August, 1916

After selling his operation on San Juan to Cowell, James McCurdy, together with Nathan Gregg and J. C. Brittain, filed for incorporation of the McCurdy Lime Company, headquartered in Eastsound, in July of 1888. But by September Gregg and his wife Maggie had filed suit against the others for not fulfilling their obligations. What subsequently became known as "Gregg's Lime Kiln" lasted only a few years. Nearby, an 1892 map indicates operations run by the "Bowen Bros. & Jamieson" and "Dailey & Boyd." Port Langdon, on the east shore of East Sound, also passed through the hands of several owners. On the west side of Orcas, at least two small operations flourished for a brief period: the Eagle Lime Company (1900-ca. 1910) and the Island Lime Company (1900-ca.1907).

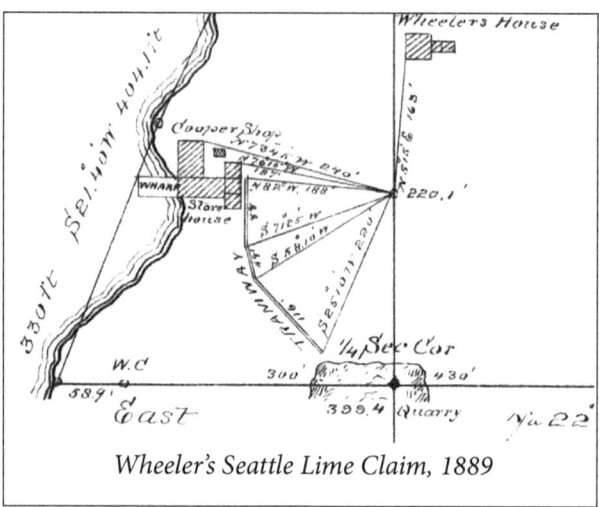

Wheeler's Seattle Lime Claim, 1889

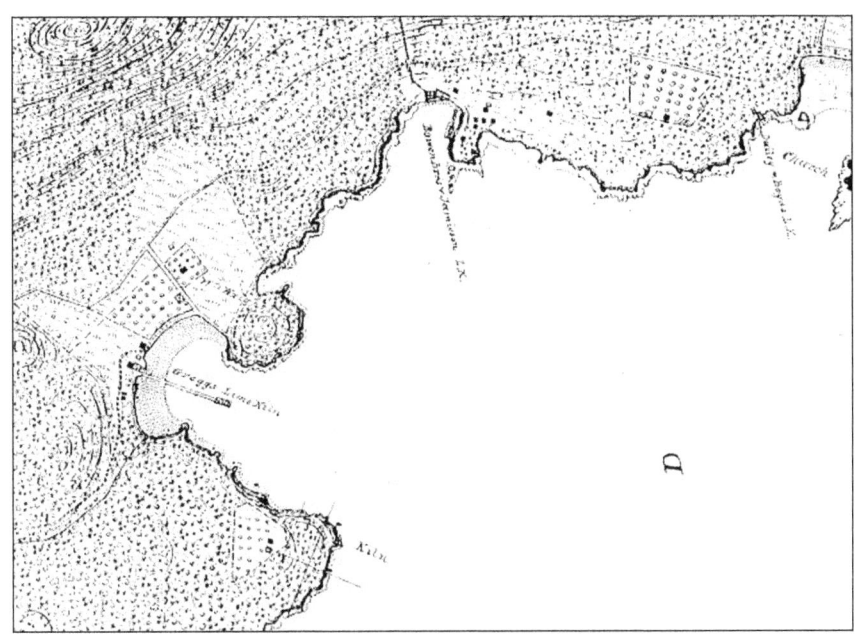
Lime Kilns in East Sound, Orcas Island, 1889

SMALL TIME PRODUCTION

A review of the 1870 and 1880 federal censuses gives a feeling for early lime production in the islands, as well as the typical business operations of these small kilns. According to the Special Manufacture Census of 1870, San Juan Lime Company produced $26,000 worth of lime—13,000 barrels at $2 a barrel—and employed 18 men for six months of a year for a total payroll of $11,000. These included a lime maker, two coopers, two carpenters, four quarrymen, a chopper, three laborers, and two cooks. Port Langdon, listed as "Shotwell & Company," had $7,000 in capital, 25 employees ($9,000 in wages), and produced 8,000 barrels in six months, for a value of $16,000 at the going rate of $2/barrel. By the time of the 1880 census, McCurdy's was producing only $18,000 of lime, and paid $6,000 to the 21 employees who worked there nine months of the year. The typical work day was 10 hours (9 in the winter); a day's wage for an "average day laborer" was $.75, but a "skilled mechanic" could earn as much as $3.50.

Most of the product during this period went to regional cities: Victoria, just 14 miles across Haro Strait on the southern tip of Vancouver Island, and Puget Sound ports such as Port Townsend, Seattle, and Tacoma. According to an 1878 newspaper article, of the 8,000 barrels produced by August of that year, two-thirds had been shipped to Tacoma and thence to Portland via railroad, while another 1,000 had been sent to British Columbia and other parts of the Sound.

ECONOMICS OF THE LIME INDUSTRY

The production of lime in the San Juan Islands responded to the economic development of the Pacific Northwest region, as well as trade with California and Hawaii. Puget Sound cities such as Bellingham, Everett, Seattle, and Tacoma witnessed extraordinary economic growth after the arrival of the railroads. The Northern Pacific selected Tacoma as its western terminus in 1873. In 1889, the Great Northern reached Everett, transforming it into a boom town. The railroad spurred development of industries such as mining, smelting, and papermaking, which in turn fueled the lime industry in the San Juan Islands. However, the Panic of 1893 soon dragged the local economy into another depression, from which it did not recover until the stimulus of the Klondike (Yukon) Gold Rush of 1896. Another boom period followed until the Depression of 1907. These economic booms and busts contributed to the formation, rise, and decline of many small companies of one or at most two kilns. Eventually, the economics of the lime industry led to the gradual consolidation and aggrandizement of these smaller operations into ownership by either Cowell or McMillin.

> *The future of the lime business is one of the brightest on Puget Sound. The demand is good, the profits are large, and the amount of rock available is restricted to three or four large quarries, which are practically inexhaustible, the smaller ledges being only large enough to supply one or at most two kilns for a few years.*
>
> "News of the Northwest," *The Pacific Magazine*, April 1891

USES OF LIME

Lime was used for several of the budding Puget Sound industries. Quicklime was used as a flux in smelting steel and other metals to remove impurities. The Port Langdon quarry was reworked in 1898 to provide rock for the Tacoma Smelter. Begun in 1888 as a lead smelter, the Tacoma Smelting and Refining Company reorganized under William Rust in 1890, eventually becoming the largest on the Pacific Coast. In 1905 Rust sold the property to the American Smelting and Refining Corporation (ASARCO), which turned it into a copper smelting and refining plant. In Everett, the Puget Sound Reduction Company had been formed by Rockefeller interests as part of the Great Northern Railroad's development of the city. In 1903, this smelter, as well as the Monte Cristo mines, was sold to ASARCO, which operated the facility intermittently until 1912.

"Paper rock" was lime used for processing the pulp (cellulose) in the papermaking process. Several pulp mills were established in the Puget Sound region. One of the earliest was the Puget Sound Pulp and Paper Company mill, constructed in 1889 in Lowell (Everett). This was joined by the Soundview (1931) and Weyerhaeuser Mill A (1936) to form the 'Big Three' pulp and paper producers in the city. On the Olympic Peninsula, the Crescent Boxboard Company, which began operations in Port Angeles in 1919, was joined a year later by the Zellerbach Company's Washington Pulp and Paper Corporation. To the north, in Bellingham, the Puget Sound Pulp and Timber Company was assembled from companies throughout the Puget Sound; during the Great Depression the plant was sold to Soundview Paper Company. In the 1950s and 1960s, several of these companies merged into larger corporations such as Scott Paper, Crown Zellerbach, and Georgia Pacific. All of them used lime or limestone from the San Juan Islands.

It is expected that the annexation of Hawaii will be a great stimulus to the lime business here, through the added stimulus which such action is likely to give to sugar refining in Hawaii, in which great quantifies of lime are used, and the Roche Harbor lime is said to be the very best obtainable in the world for this purpose.

San Juan Islander, June 23, 1898

Hawaiian plantations used lime from the San Juan Islands as "sugar rock" in the refining process. Lime was also used as a source of fertilizer in the sugar cane fields. Ships bearing barrels of lime for the sugar plantations sailed from the San Juans to Hawaii on a regular basis.

Hauling cordwood, San Juan Island

MAKING LIME

Quarrying limestone was heavy, loud, and dusty work that required a great deal of strength and endurance. "Powdermen" blew the limestone free from cliffs with explosives and then "breakers" split up the larger boulders. Men who "broke rock" were described as solidly built with sinewy arms, able to wield jackhammers skillfully and repeatedly, knowing where the fissures were and how to strike them just right so as to split the rocks into the right size pieces (usually 8-12" in diameter). One of the twentieth century innovations was the compressed air (pneumatic) drill, which was used to drill the holes for the explosive charges, as well as breaking up the large boulders. Then they had to haul the rock to the top of the kilns, which involved either leading a team of horses pulling carts on rails or sending the ore in buckets down a tram or funicular. The quarried limestone could then be either shipped unprocessed or 'burned' in the kilns to produce lime.

Wood—principally old growth Douglas fir—was the fuel used to 'burn' limestone. Cut into four-foot long split logs called "cordwood," it took about 3-4 cords to fire a kiln continuously through a 24-hour period. (A cord is a 4' by 4' by 8' stack of wood.) Wood was supplied by woodcutters and farmers clearing their land on Lopez, Orcas, and San Juan, as well as many of the nearby smaller islands, and hauled by wagon or shipped by scow to the kiln sites. Every kiln operation had several wood cutters who provided fuel for the kilns. Wood cutters made from $1.50 to $1.75 per cord, and a good woodman could cut 1½ cords a day.

> For the badly twisted timber of these windswept islands is the very hardest wood to cut or split that I have ever seen. So when my first day's work was done and the result was one half cord of wood and ten full sized blisters on my hands and scarcely able to drag my aching bones back to the cookhouse, or to eat after I got there, I began to realize the full beauty of cord wood cutting on Orcas Island for a living.
>
> —Diary of James Tulloch

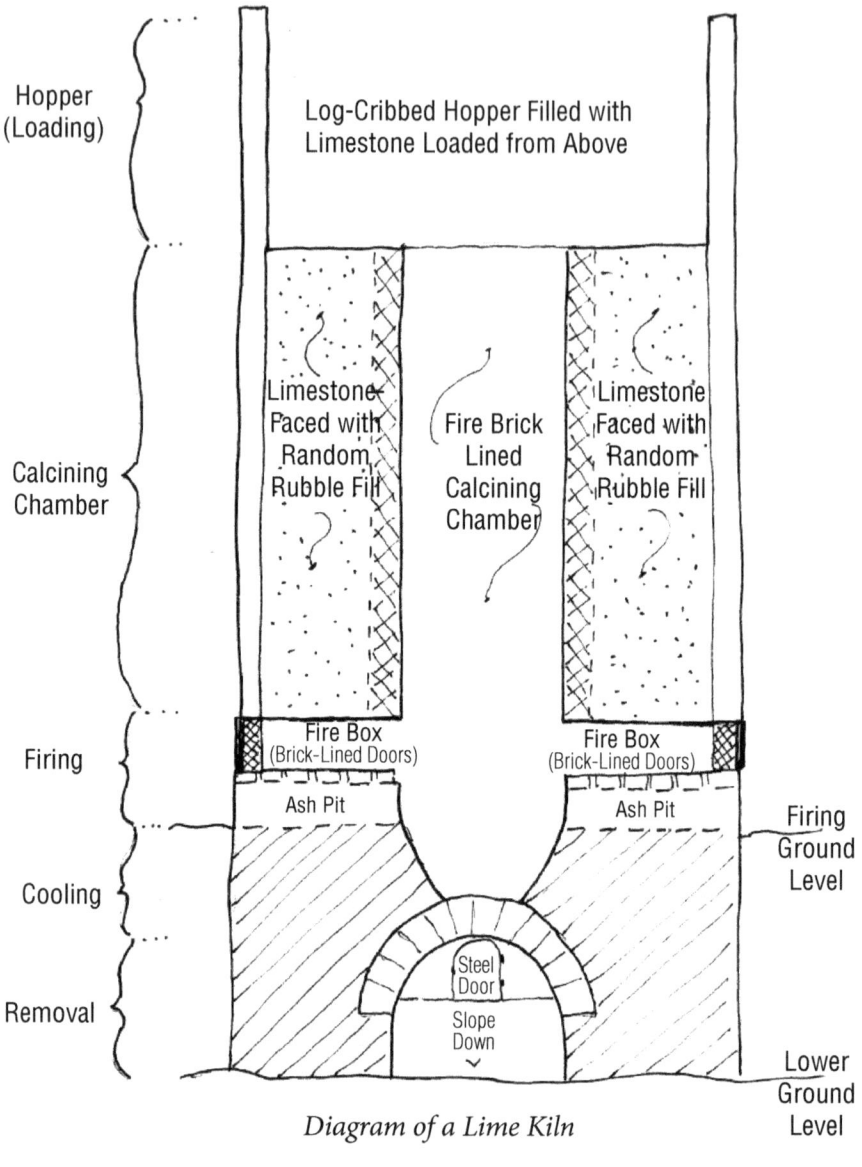

Diagram of a Lime Kiln

calcium carbonate $\xrightarrow{\text{heat}}$ calcium oxide + carbon dioxide
($CaCO_3$) (CaO) (CO_2)
LIME

Stoking the Kilns, Roche Harbor, San Juan Island

A lime kiln was a three-level stone structure approximately 30' high and 18' square with a brick-lined, cylinder-shaped chamber inside. The top level—sometimes a log crib—had an opening at the top into which the quarried limestone was loaded, having been split into rocks (usually 8-12" in diameter) by quarrymen. One load of rocks for a large kiln would weigh about 15 tons.

The middle level had fireboxes, about 18" wide by 24" high and lined with firebrick, on both sides of the kiln, open to the interior chamber. Here the firemen, working twelve-hour shifts, fired the kiln with cordwood and maintained the proper temperature (keeping it hot but not too hot—around 1800° F). The wood did not come into contact with the limestone; the heat from the fireboxes passed upward through the stone, driving off the carbon dioxide (CO_2) from the calcium carbonate ($CaCO_3$) to form lime: calcium oxide (CaO).

The lower level was where workers raked out the burnt rock, still in large chunks (8-12" in diameter), about every 3-4 hours, with an average draw of 12-15 barrels. They used long (10-12') rods to channel the burnt rock from the bottom of the chamber into a chute. After the lime chunks had cooled, they were packed in barrels, whose heads were sealed in order to keep the lime from hydrating once again. Barrels were assembled at a cooperage located close to the kilns, so they were readily accessible for packing.

Barreling the Lime, Roche Harbor, San Juan Island

The barrels, weighing between 200 and 250 pounds each, were then put on a funicular or loaded on a flatbed wagon on tracks that was drawn by horses to warehouses near the wharf, where they could be stored until shipped to market. Workers took great pride in being able to stack the heavy barrels three layers high.

DANGEROUS CARGO

Ships laden with barrels of lime, some stacked on open decks, were carrying a very dangerous cargo since quicklime that becomes wet generates high heat. The list of ships that suffered severe damage or sank as the result of fires ignited by their lime cargo is a long one. One of the earliest and most well-known ships in Puget Sound, the *General Harney*, which helped haul troops and supplies from Fort Townsend to San Juan Island during the Pig War, caught fire with a cargo of lime in 1876 and had to be beached. The Roche Harbor Lime Company fleet was not immune: the *William G. Irvin*, loaded with a $30,000 cargo of lime, was scuttled in San Francisco Bay after a month's efforts to quell the smoldering pile, and even the *Archer*, an iron-hulled barkentine, burned and sank while carrying a full load of lime.

Two of the most harrowing incidents involved ships hauling lime as freight along with passengers. On November 10, 1889, the *J. B. Libby* was on her way to Port Townsend, transporting 500 barrels of lime from Roche Harbor, when she encountered rough water and lost her rudder. The ship's captain was trying to run the boat onto the shore at Smith Island when fire was discovered in the hold filled with lime. Passengers scrambled into lifeboats, and were rescued a few hours later by a passing steam schooner. The burned hull of the *J. B. Libby* was eventually towed into Port Townsend. The sinking of the *T. W. Lake* on December 5, 1923, was even worse. Sailing from Roche Harbor to Anacortes with a cargo of 300 barrels of lime, she was caught in 72-mile-an-hour winds in Rosario Strait. The ship sank, with the entire 15-man crew lost. After recovering their bodies, it was discovered that all but one had worn life vests; furthermore, two of the men's watches had stopped, one at 7:13 p.m. and the other 7:20 p.m., helping investigators ascertain when the disaster occurred. As a result of this and other incidents of fire and subsequent loss of life and property, the U. S. Coast Guard prohibited ships carrying passengers from carrying hazardous cargo like lime.

Barreled Lime Ready to be Shipped, Roche Harbor, San Juan Island

LIFE AT THE LIME KILNS

The men who worked at the lime kilns were of mixed ethnicity and nationality. Industrialists took advantage of the various immigrant groups that came to America for work, so the lime kiln populations changed over time. Early on, the majority of workers were English, Irish, or Welsh, with a strong contingent of Cornish quarrymen and Chinese cooks. In the 1890s and 1900s, many Japanese worked at Roche Harbor. However, by 1910 the nationalities of the workers had shifted: census takers enumerated many "Austrians"—actually from Croatia, part of the Austrian-Hungarian Empire at the time—at Cowell's and Scandinavians and "Russians"—actually Germans from the Lower Volga—at Roche Harbor.

Because most lime kilns were located in areas that were not near other settlements in the islands, companies often provided housing and meals for the men working there. The boarding house at the San Juan Lime Company was typical: a large, two story frame building that included a kitchen, dining hall, store, and superin-

Workers' Cottages and Dormatories, Roche Harbor, San Juan Island

Lime Kiln and Quarry Crew, Cowell's, San Juan Island

tendent's residence downstairs and bunk rooms upstairs. Several lime kiln operations served as community centers by providing stores for supplies and post offices for mail. Eureka had a post office, named "Werner," for the brief period from 1890 to 1892, as well as a hotel, saloon, two bunk houses, and several cabins. Roche Harbor became a small village, including residences for management and workers, a hotel, store, church, school, and doctor's office. Lime companies were foremost in adopting technological innovations such as electrical power and telephone systems.

> *There will be a "Hard Times Ball" at the Union Grove hall, Friday, the 28th, under the auspices of "Cowell's Lime Kiln Club." Every body is cordially invited to come and have a good time. A hard times supper will be served at midnight. First class music by the San Juan Orchestra. Tickets, including supper, 75 cents. There will be no white shirts allowed.*
>
> —*San Juan Islander,* 1894

COWELL v. MCMILLIN

In 1906, E. V. (Ernest) Cowell, the son of Henry Cowell, brought John S. McMillin to court over the dealings of the Tacoma and Roche Harbor Lime Company. This was the culmination of a bitter feud between the elder Cowell and McMillin. The lawsuit not only offers insight into the specific history of the two men and their companies, but also provides a window into the business practices of the time: monopolistic control of markets, price fixing and undercutting, and manipulation of corporate structure.

The Cowells held shares in the Tacoma and Roche Harbor Lime Company, but not a controlling interest. E. V. Cowell claimed that McMillin had formed the company through fraudulent means (by liquidating the assets of the Tacoma Lime Company); that he received an excessive salary—determined by himself—as manager; and that operations and activities of the Staveless Barrel Company were improper and irregular, resulting in a loss of dividends for stockholders.

John S. McMillin Touting His Wares

In 1849 Henry Cowell arrived at San Francisco during the height of the California Gold Rush. He first captured the drayage and storage market, and then in 1865, along with Isaac Davis, bought a share in a lime manufacturing concern in Santa Cruz. Cowell moved there to supervise the new firm of Davis & Cowell. In 1888, Cowell acquired Davis's share, thus becoming the sole owner of the largest lime manufacturing empire (the Cowell Lime & Cement Company) in California, and therefore the West Coast—except for Roche Harbor.

> *[Ernest Cowell] reveals himself in the attitude of a would-be destroyer of a business competitor through the instrumentality of judicial process.*
>
> —U. S. District Court Judge C. H. Hanford (Court Case No. 1413)

John S. McMillin, who founded the Tacoma and Roche Harbor Lime Company, grew up in limestone-rich Indiana. In 1882 he moved to Tacoma, where he was first involved with lime in the Puyallup Valley. In 1883, the Tacoma Lime Company incorporated; McMillin later relied upon both its assets and the economic and political support of its directors as well as other businessmen in the Tacoma area.

Stemming from an initial dispute between Henry Cowell and McMillin over the purchase of the Roche Harbor lime works on San Juan Island, and therefore ultimate control of the Pacific Northwest lime industry, the lawsuit was the culmination of a continuing feud. Skirmishes had already been fought over ownership of nearby Lime Kiln (McCurdy's), but they were exacerbated by McMillin's business practices at Roche Harbor. McMillin had basic controlling interest of the Tacoma and Roche Harbor Lime Company: 341 shares, compared to Cowell's 167. McMillin's salary, according to his own testimony, was first fixed at $2,500 per annum, and then rose to $3,000 in 1889, doubled to $6,000 two years later, and then doubled again to a whopping $12,000 in 1895—two years into one of the worst depressions in U. S. history. In the meantime, although there were substantial profits from the operation, the company issued no dividends until 1903.

COMPETITION AND CONTROVERSY

John S. McMillin was the Tacoma and Roche Harbor Lime Company. It was largely through his sound business acumen that he was able to turn a middling operation into the largest lime works in the Pacific Northwest, and thus challenge Henry Cowell, the "Lime King" of the West Coast. He was able to do this through near dictatorial power at Roche Harbor and through ruthless business practices typical of the "Robber Baron" era. Among these were price fixing and monopolistic control of the market at a time when the demand for lime first saw unprecedented opportunity and then a precipitous decline following the Depression of 1893.

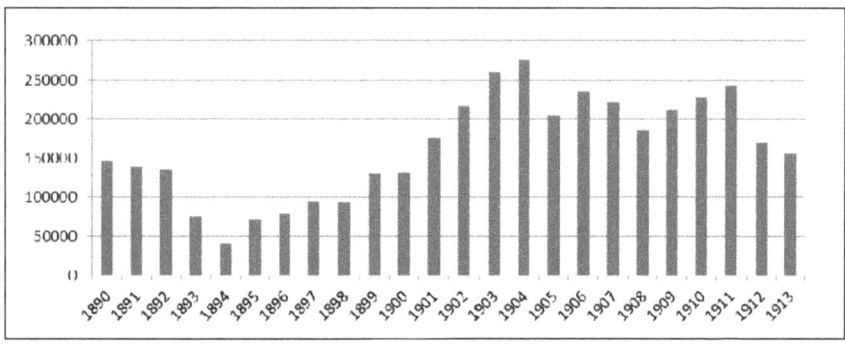

Annual Sales of Roche Harbor Lime (in Barrels), 1890 - 1913

During the 1880s, the population of the Pacific Northwest swelled by a phenomenal 165 percent, primarily in four urban areas: Portland, Seattle, Spokane, and Tacoma. By 1910, one-third of the entire population of Oregon, Washington, and Idaho lived in these four cities. Devastating fires in Ellensburg, Seattle, and Spokane in 1889 brought about changes in attitude about building safety, resulting in new construction techniques. Buildings constructed of brick with lime mortar were erected in place of the wood structures easily consumed by fire. This generated an enormous demand for lime as mortar in the Pacific Northwest as well as the entire West Coast.

Prior to the legislation of the Progressive Era "Trust-busters," lime manufacturers, in common with other industries, colluded to set fixed prices for the commodity itself, the minimum required lot size for purchase, and freight or shipping charges. In July of 1900 McMillin drafted a proposed contract for all lime manufacturers in the State of Washington. Under the terms of the agreement, producers would sell lime for no less than $1.25 per barrel. This price was reserved for dealers or agents who bought in lots of 100 barrels or more, with the exception of dealers in Whatcom and Snohomish counties, where the minimum lot size was 50 barrels. McMillin's proposal went on to include a different price for dealers not described in the contract: $1.50 per barrel with the supplier assuming the shipping costs from point of departure to destination. No rebates or discounts were to be allowed, nor would any manufacturer be allowed to purchase any empty second-hand barrels.

However, McMillin proceeded to underbid the fixed prices that he helped establish. The Panic of 1893, which originated with the collapse of the railroad and banking industries, precipitated an almost decade-long national depression that hit the West Coast particularly hard. During this period, there was little to no construction, so lime manufacturers, among other building material suppliers, competed fiercely for major government projects. George Willey, an agent for both Cowell and McMillin, testified that McMillin secured the contract for one of the state university buildings by going below the established price for the sale of lime prevailing in Puget Sound. This initiated the "Lime War," a four-year period following the Panic of 1893, when the price of lime was anything but uniform. In 1891 the retail price of lime in Western Washington was $1.60 per barrel; by 1904, the price had dropped to less than a dollar per barrel.

Staveless Barrel Factory at Roche Harbor, San Juan Island

Fir and cedar logs are cut into pieces the length of the barrels desired and then revolved against a knife so constructed that a shaving the proper shape, thickness, and bevel is pared off, ready to be made into a barrel.

The San Juan Islands Illustrated Supplement to the *San Juan Islander*, 1901

Another means of dominating the market was through vertical integration: controlling the lime industry from quarrying, through processing, barreling, and warehousing, to shipping. McMillin focused on barreling when he established a staveless barrel plant in 1891. The "staveless barrel" was based upon a method developed by the Waterman-Chapman Barrel Machine Company, whereby machines shaved a thick veneer for the two halves of a barrel, resulting in just two staves and joints, as opposed to a regular barrel of seventeen staves and joints. McMillin purchased rights to the process in 1891, but a fire on September 10, 1892 destroyed the plant he had built at Roche Harbor. The "Staveless Barrel Company" was incorporated in Tacoma at the end of December 1894, and McMillin sold his rights to the company.

However, principal ownership of the company remained in the family, because his wife Louella held the majority of stock through mortgaging some of her estate holdings. William Shultz, secretary and stockholder of the Tacoma and Roche Harbor Lime Company, was vice president and trustee, as well as bookkeeper, of the Staveless Barrel Company. The cost of a barrel prior to 1893 was 32½ cents; the contract set a new price of 30 cents each, but with a 1½-cent royalty to McMillin.

McMillin used the barreling operation as a means of establishing a shadow corporation that was able to generate income and, in particular, transfer the profit to himself, thus sidestepping the Cowells' interest in the principal corporation, the Tacoma and Roche Harbor Lime Company. According to testimony, although the Staveless Barrel Company did not issue a dividend until 1896, some $7,000-21,000 per annum was paid out; in addition, over this ten-year period McMillin was paid approximately $125,000 for management.

PORTLAND CEMENT

In the early 1900s, lime production changed in response to the growing importance of Portland cement. Although cement has ancient origins, the late 1890s and early 1900s saw its growing use in mid- to high-rise commercial and industrial structures. On nearby Vancouver Island in British Columbia, the Vancouver Portland Cement Company, under Robert P. Butchart, had established a plant at Tod Inlet in 1904. McMillin developed plans for manufacturing Portland cement at Roche Harbor, seeking capital and partners from Canada and the East Coast. Blueprints dated June 1903 delineate a hugely ambitious scheme to convert the existing plant into a Portland cement operation. The Roche Harbor Lime and Cement Company incorporated on November 2, 1905.

McMillin cultivated both a business and social relationship with Butchart. On behalf of a number of prospective business partners from Eastern Canada, Butchart began negotiations with McMillin to purchase his stock in the Tacoma and Roche Harbor

Bagging Lime at Roche Harbor, San Juan Island

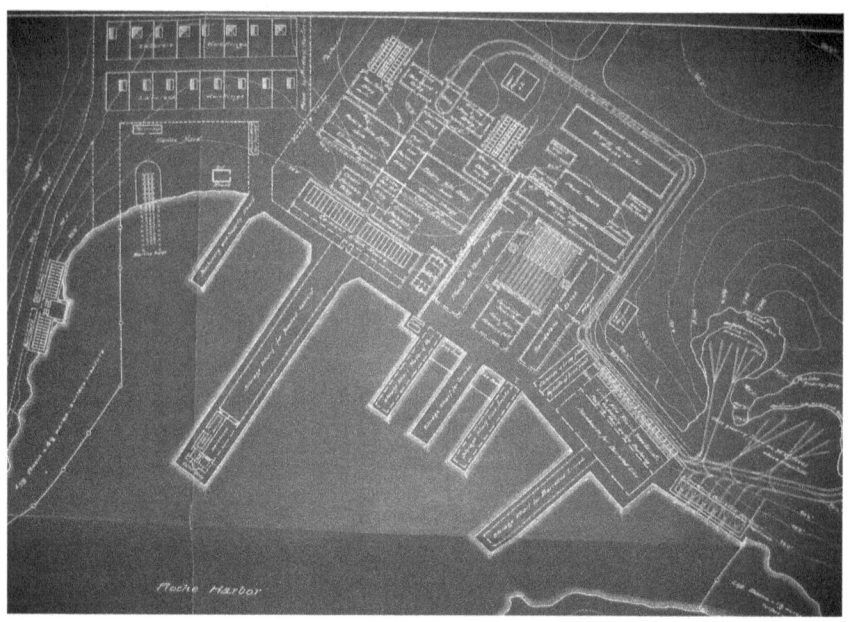

Plan for Portland Cement Plant at Roche Harbor, 1906

Lime Company. Their intention was to develop a large Portland cement manufacturing plant with the capacity of 5,000 barrels a day. In addition to acquiring McMillin's stock, the consortium sought to buy out all remaining stockholders. Blocked by E. V. Cowell, who refused to dispose of his 309 shares, Butchart and his associates scuttled their plans. They declined to purchase McMillin's stock, effectively leaving him without the capital and wherewithal to modernize and build the facility.

During the course of the lawsuit McMillin had been enjoined from selling or transferring the property itself, its assets and business, and the capital stock or shares in the Tacoma and Roche Harbor Lime Company, a further blow to his plans to modernize and become a player in the burgeoning and lucrative cement industry. When the judge issued his decree in 1909, he dismissed Cowell's complaint and exonerated McMillin. In the meantime, in 1906 Ernest Cowell had begun construction in California of the "greatest cement plant on the Pacific coast." The Cowell Portland Cement Company plant, comprising eight oil-fired rotary kilns on a 2,000 acre site, opened in February of 1908.

DEPRESSION AND DECLINE

Following the defeat of McMillin's plans for Portland cement production, Roche Harbor suffered a series of vicissitudes during the 1920s and 1930s. On July 28, 1923, a fire swept through the works, destroying the kilns, warehouses, store, and wharf. McMillin responded quickly, and apparently had the kilns operating within a few days. He rebuilt the wharf, with a new store, office, community hall, and yacht club. A close look at Roche Harbor's production charts indicates declines around the time of World War I, at the onset of the Great Depression, and during World War II. (An exception appears to be 1937, which may have coincided with the construction of Grand Coulee Dam, the largest concrete structure in the world at the time.)

Except for Roche Harbor, the kilns at most limestone operations in the San Juan Islands were shut down permanently in the 1930s. The kilns' closure coincided with the Great Depression when the demand for lime declined severely. Also contributing to the closing of the lime works was antiquated or outdated technology. The processing of lime in the San Juan Islands had not changed significantly in almost 60 years. It was inefficient, labor-intensive,

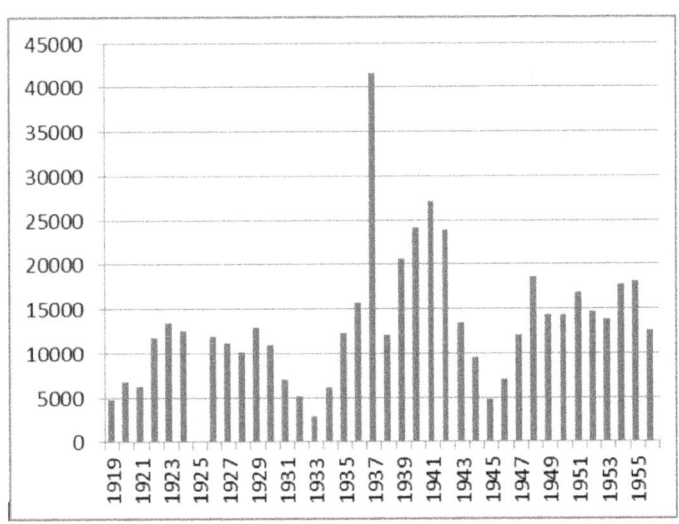

Annual Sales of Roche Harbor Lime (in Tons), 1919 - 1956

and therefore not cost-effective to continue operations. Moreover, the deposits of high quality limestone located in the quarries near most of the kilns had been exhausted. The lower grade rock was too far away, requiring more labor and materials to haul it down the slope to the kilns.

Loading Lime on Ship, Roche Harbor, San Juan Island, 1925

Shipping costs rose, and fewer ships sailed the waters of Puget Sound. Freight bound for West Coast cities was primarily being sent by rail. There was some market for agricultural lime in Eastern Washington, which meant it was packaged in sacks and hauled by barge or scows to Everett where it could easily be transferred to rail cars. The remaining lime was destined for pulp mills in Puget Sound. Lime manufacture continued until the onset of the Great Depression, reaching a nadir in 1933. During the 1940s and early 1950s, production gradually shifted to paper rock. Operations lasted the longest at Roche Harbor, until 1956, when the property was bought and converted into a resort.

LEGACY

By the time (1959-1960) geologist Wilbert R. Danner surveyed kiln and quarry sites in the San Juan Islands for his *Limestone Resources of Western Washington*, none were actively producing lime and only a handful were being quarried, mostly for paper rock. On San Juan, ten quarries were identified, but none of them were operational; on Orcas, of the thirty or so known quarries only three had been active during the recent past; and the scattering of quarries on Cliff, Crane, Henry, and Shaw had ceased operations decades before. What remains today is a legacy of the extensive lime industry which was so vital to the economy of the San Juan Islands and the Pacific Northwest.

> *Roche Harbor is a perfect land-locked harbor with good anchorage... The scenery is most picturesque, and only the fact that the Tacoma & Roche Harbor Lime Co. own all the land, and will not part with it, has prevented it from becoming a popular resort.*
>
> —Capt. J. J. Gilbert, U. S. Coast and Geodetic Survey, 1894

Roche Harbor, San Juan Island, 1940s

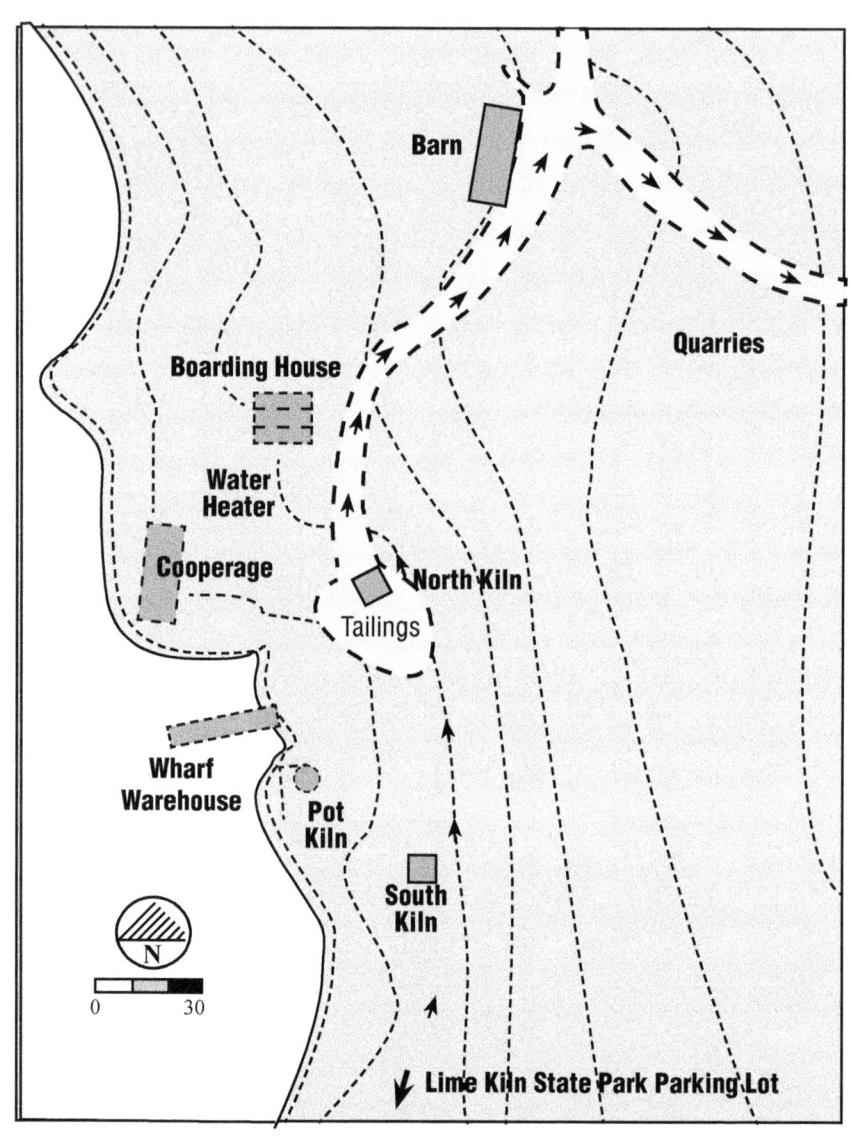

*Lime Kiln Quarries and Kilns
San Juan Island, Washington*

TOUR GUIDE

LIME KILN
San Juan Lime Company • *McCurdy's* • *Cowell's*
San Juan Island

Lime Kiln is the site of the earliest and longest-operating limestone quarrying and lime manufacture in the San Juan Islands. Included among the remains from these operations are two lime kilns—one restored and one in ruins—as well as a large assemblage of archaeological features. The site is owned by the State of Washington—Lime Kiln Point State Park—and the San Juan County Land Bank—Limekiln Preserve.

Directions. From Friday Harbor, proceed south on Spring Street out of town for 1.7 miles; turn left onto Douglas Road, which changes to Bailer Hill Road (3.5 miles) and Westside Road (7.5). Park at Lime Kiln Point State Park (9 miles).

History. Limestone was first discovered and assayed here by the North West Boundary Commission during the Pig War (1859), and Lyman Cutlar, the man who shot the pig, was one of the three developers who first manufactured lime here. Limestone was quarried and lime was produced in the kilns at Lime Kiln for a period of 75 years: as the San Juan Lime Company from 1860 until 1886, when Henry Cowell purchased the operations, and it became known as Cowell's. After 1935, the lime operations ceased, but Cowell's continued quarrying limestone until 1957. Once the kilns were closed and the quarrying ceased, the site remained undeveloped for many years. Lime Kiln Point State Park was established in 1984 from Coast Guard land that had been set aside for the Lime Kiln Light House (established in 1914; constructed in 1919). In 1997 the San Juan County Land Bank purchased the surrounding land, along with Deadman Bay and a stretch of open cliff extending south along the shore from Lime Kiln.

*San Juan Lime Company (Lime Kiln)
Pre-1888 (above)
and 2013 (below)*

Description. There are upwards of 4 miles of trails in the State Park and Preserve. Walking from the Parking Area, you will see the Visitors Center and 2 trails: one leading to the water and the other in back of the Visitors Center which is a 1.5 mile loop that takes you past the lighthouse keeper's residence to a viewpoint overlooking the lime works, and then past the two kilns and up into the quarries. The limestone deposits that supported the operations on the site consisted of three large, lens-like beds as well as smaller pods, which extended from sea level to over 320 feet in elevation. The first quarries to be mined were concentrated in several bench-like areas around 200-260 feet above sea level, with the processing, storage, shipping, and living areas located on the slopes below. An overall system of gravitational flow from upslope to downslope determined the design and arrangement of the structures on the site. After being quarried, the stone chunks were loaded by hand onto carts on temporary railroad tracks and transported via log trestles to the top of the kilns (at about 60 feet above sea level), which were built into the hillside. The limestone was heated by means of fireboxes midway down on the sides, and the lime was removed from the bottom and packed in barrels. The cooperage, warehouse, and wharf were all located near the water's edge or on the cliffs immediately proximate thereto. Supporting structures, such as the boarding house, barn, stable, office, and connecting roadbeds, were located in the middle level, close to the processing areas. Starting from the overlook at the northern edge of the State Park, you will encounter structures in reverse order from the operations, working uphill from the wharf area to the kilns, warehouses, boarding house, and barn/stable until you arrive at the quarries above.

The first structure you encounter is the ***South Kiln***, referred to by island old-timers as the "Little Kiln"—a tall masonry shaft built into the hillside. Restored in 1999 by Washington State Parks, it offers an interesting contrast to the unrestored North Kiln further along the trail on the Land Bank property. The South Kiln was constructed of an inner lining of two courses of firebrick around a flattened oval, contained in squared outer walls of rough limestone with rubble fill in between. Large timber frame beams, held in place with metal tie rods, were used to brace the structure. Sandstone, quarried from nearby Sucia Island, was used in key places such as the arch over the bottom removal area as well as the quoins (corner stones) of the shaft. The paired fireboxes are located on the north and south sides of the kiln; open-brickwork grates on the bottom let the ashes fall into the cinder boxes below for easy removal. At the very base of the structure is an arched opening for removal and barreling of the lime.

Downslope of the South Kiln are the remains of a rock and mortar foundation wall and a pit or depression with a slightly raised "lip." Currently filled with rubble, this may have been the site of a **Pot Kiln**, an early form of lime kiln comprising a brick-lined hole that was filled with limestone and fuel (wood) for a one-time firing. Below this at the water's edge of the ravine are the scattered remains of what historic photographs indicate were an extensive complex of **Wharfage** and **Warehouses**. The wharf extended at least 40-50 feet out from the shore, and consisted of a loading area with a crane hoist as well as storage or processing sheds. According to old-time islanders, a large storm in the 1920s washed out the wharf. All that remains are several iron rings driven into or cemented onto the rocks near the water, as well as some concrete pads that probably served as the foundation of pilings for the wharfs and supporting structures for the buildings. Several round pilings can still be seen embedded in the ground in the tidal area. Across the ravine at the top of the cliff can be seen the foundation wall of the **Cooperage**, which historic photographs indicate was a long, gable-roofed structure with barrels full of water atop the ridge, which served as fire suppression.

On the water's edge and between the South and North kilns are **Tailings**, or remains of discarded partially-burnt limestone. Tailings were placed underneath the foundations of several of the buildings at Lime Kiln, such as the nearby Boarding House, where they were used to create a level platform for the structure.

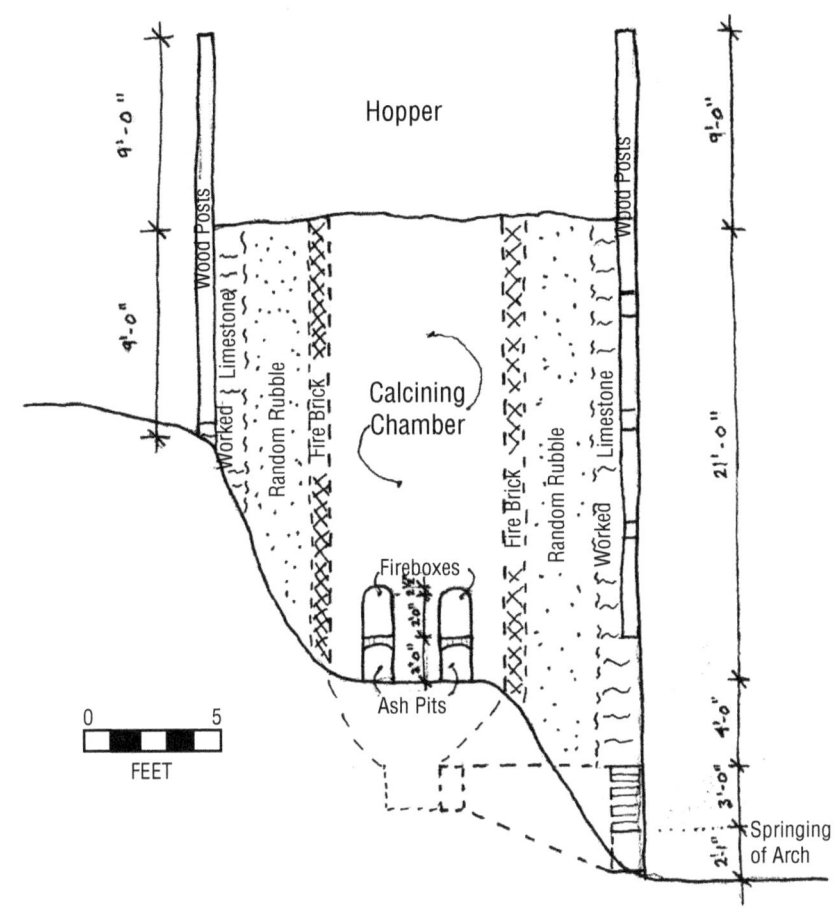

Section through North Kiln, Lime Kiln

Like the South Kiln, the **North Kiln** is a tall masonry shaft built into the hillside, measuring approximately 18' high on the upslope side and 30' on the down slope, and 18' wide (on the lime-removal side) and 20' (on the firebox sides). A wooden superstructure, rising another 9' above the top of the stone shaft, was used as the hopper for the limestone prior to its descent into the calcining chamber. This chamber, which is exposed on the south side, is constructed of an inner lining of two courses of firebrick around an oval that measures approximately 6' wide by 8' long, contained within squared outer walls of rough limestone and rubble fill (including, in some cases, chunks of burnt firebrick from old linings) in between. This structure was held together by 6"x 8" vertical wood columns that were mortised into the top 9' of the corners of the masonry shaft. Large (6"x 8") timber frame beams, set at 5'-6' intervals, as well as 1½"-diameter tie rods were used to stabilize the structure. Like the South Kiln, Sucia Island sandstone was used in key places such as the arches over the bottom removal area as well as quoins of the shaft. The fireboxes, although less intact, are similar to those in the South Kiln.

Farther along, the remains of the **Boarding House**, roughly 33' wide by 36' long, sits upon a hillside that slopes down to the water. It consisted of two parts: a one-story, shed-roofed section to the north and a two-story, gable-roofed section to the south. The shed-roofed section contained three rooms: a kitchen to the northeast next to two rooms of unknown use. The ground floor of the second story section boasted a 19½' wide by 24' long dining hall and what may have been a store to the west (water side). The second story contained three rooms, each approximately 11-12' wide by 19½' long; these were all used as a dormitory or sleeping quarters. Because of its deteriorated condition, which posed a serious danger to visitors to the site, in 2005 the standing walls of the boarding house were induced to collapse upon themselves, and the resulting ruin fenced off. Near the Boarding House is a small structure, which contains a metal barrel set on its side, surrounded by concrete and firebrick. Because of its proximity to the Boarding House, it is conjectured that this served as a **Water Heater** for the kitchen in that structure.

Further along the trail are the remains of a **Barn**, consisting of a stone foundation with scattered wooden posts, beams, and joists. Historic photographs indicate that there were at least two successive buildings at this location, the later being a large gable-roofed structure. The wooden remains indicate that the upper portion of the building was a timber frame structure, used as a stable for the horses that hauled the limestone and storage for their hay.

On the next level up are the limestone deposits, which consisted of three large, irregular, lenticular beds ranging from 800-

1,500 feet in length and 50-300 feet in width, as well as 11 smaller (less than 100 feet in length and 50 feet in width) pods. Although these deposits extend from sea level to over 320 feet in altitude, the worked **Quarries** are concentrated in bench-like areas around 200-320 feet above sea level. They appear as large, amphitheater-like spaces where the limestone has been worked from the surrounding stone walls. Massive piles of both scree and tailings form talus-like slopes at the base of these cliff walls and downslope of the level bench areas. There are some artifacts, such as worked logs and sections of railroad track, scattered in these areas. On the cliffs above the quarry walls you can see several of the drilled holes that were used to place explosives to blast huge segments of the stone from the cliff face to the quarry floor below.

North Kiln and Boarding House, Lime Kiln, 1959

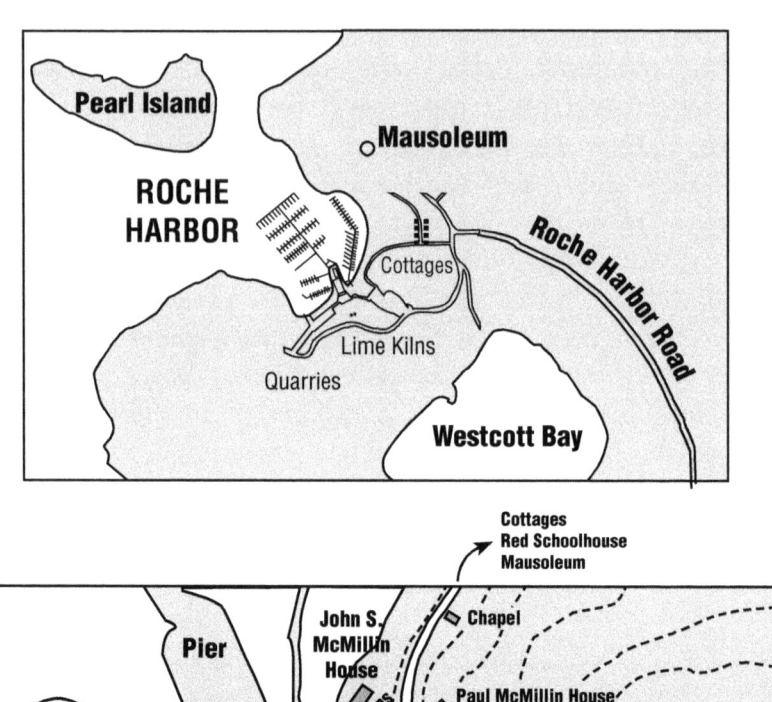

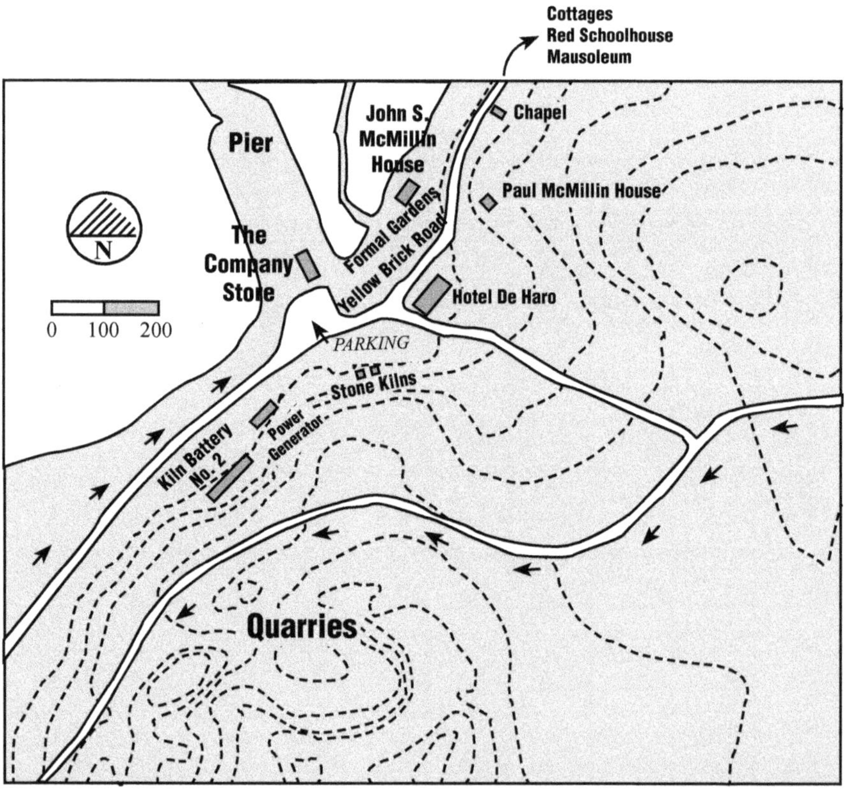

*Roche Harbor Quarries and Kilns
San Juan Island, Washington*

TOUR GUIDE

ROCHE HARBOR
Tacoma and Roche Harbor Lime Company
Roche Harbor Lime and Cement Company
San Juan Island

Roche Harbor was not only the most extensive lime manufacturing site but also features the largest collection of publicly-accessible lime production features in the San Juan Islands. At one time the town of Roche Harbor had some 800 residents and the company assets included 15 quarries, 13 kilns, a railroad, a power plant, cooperages, warehouses, piers, a post office, a store, a hotel, a doctor's clinic, and residences for the owners and workers.

Directions. From Friday Harbor, on Spring Street turn right onto Second Street, turn right on Tucker Avenue (.4 miles), which becomes Roche Harbor Road; at the end (8.8 miles) is the gateway to Roche Harbor Resort. Or, from Spring Street, turn right on Second Street, which becomes Guard (.7 miles), Beaverton Valley Road (3.5 miles), and West Valley Road (5.2 miles); after 1.3 miles, turn left on to Roche Harbor Road, which you follow to the Roche Harbor Resort gateway (1.4 miles).

History. First developed by Richard and Robert Scurr in 1879, Roche Harbor became the largest lime operation in the San Juan Islands. After John S. McMillin established the Tacoma and Roche Harbor Lime Company in 1886, it became the largest lime operation west of the Mississippi. Boasting some of the purest limestone in the Northwest from an "inexhaustible body of rock," at its height Roche Harbor's 15 quarries and two batteries of 13 lime kilns produced about 1500 200-lb. barrels of lime a day, and shipped them to ports along the West Coast and as far away as Argentina and Hawaii. In 1956, the last kilns were shut down, and under the ownership of the Tarte Family the site was converted into a 'boatel,' eventually becoming Roche Harbor Resort.

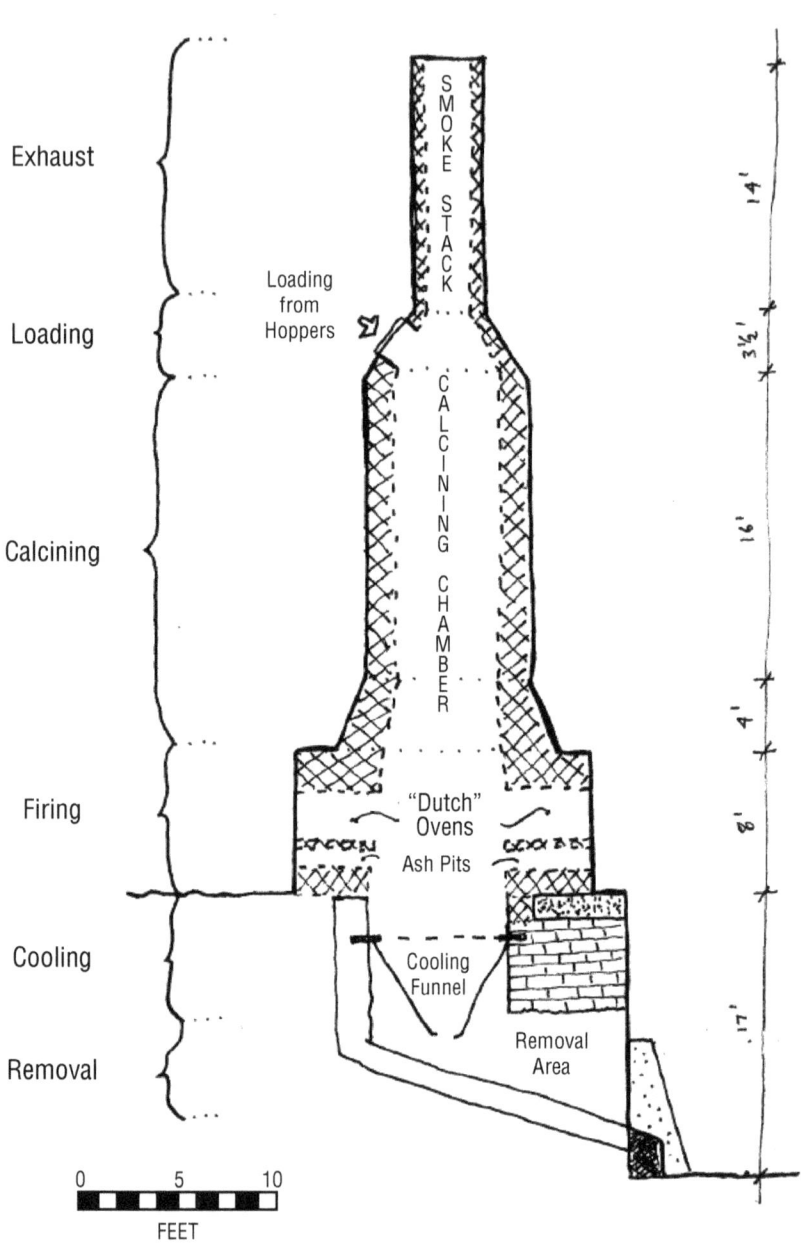

Section through "Monitor" Kiln, Battery No. 2, Roche Harbor

Description. This tour, about 2 miles on paved and dirt paths on relatively easy terrain, takes you from where the limestone was mined (the quarries) to the center of the processing (burning, barreling, and warehousing) operations, then through the various support facilities (company store and pier, hotel, residences, chapel, and school), ending at the residents' final resting places (cemetery and mausoleum).

Roche Harbor Pit Quarry

It is recommended that you first drive past the Quarries, and then park at the Resort near the Company Store for walking around the village. After that, you can drive to the parking lot near the cemetery to complete that part of the tour.

The process began with mining limestone from **Quarries**, fifteen of which were located in deposits about one-quarter of a mile wide that extend across the peninsula from Roche Harbor to Westcott Bay. Today, the Quarries that are visible from the roadway appear as a series of amphitheater-like spaces. Quarrymen drilled a series of holes in the limestone cliffs and then powdermen set charges to blow large boulders onto the quarry floor below. There other quarrymen would break the rock into 8-12"-diameter pieces and load them into horse carts (later trams on railroad tracks) and haul them to the kilns.

There were two batteries of kilns at Roche Harbor. No. 1 consisted of two older **Stone Kilns** (#3 & #4, just to the west of the new

Quarryman's Hall), built by the Scurr Brothers around 1879, and three others built by McMillin in 1886 (#1, #2 & #5—remains of #5 can be seen to the south of #3 and #4). Further south are a series of brick arches with concrete reinforcements, comprising the base of **Battery No. 2**'s 8 metal-jacketed, 'Monitor-style' or 'bottle' kilns (#6-13). After quarrying, the limestone was transported via narrow gauge railway to the hoppers at the top of the kilns, where it was calcined or 'burned,' converting the calcium carbonate ($CaCO_3$) into lime (CaO) by driving off carbon dioxide (CO_2). In order to do this, the kilns were heated to around 1800°F with wood fuel—consuming from 3½ - 4 cords a day per kiln. When cooled in the lower part of the kilns, the lime was drawn off into barrels. McMillin standardized this process by having scales at the end of iron chutes leading from the bottom of the kilns, where barrels were filled with chunks of lime until they weighed exactly 200 pounds.

Near Battery No. 2 is the **Generator Plant**, which used Morse-Fairbanks diesel-fired generators to power Roche Harbor, one of the first communities in the islands to have electricity. A 150-horse

Roche Harbor Railroad Supplying Limestone to Kilns

Roche Harbor Company Town & Hotel de Haro

power, two cycle engine originally provided power to the lime plant by using belts from the engine. It was replaced in the 1930s by a larger 225-horse power, three cylinder engine with direct drive shafts. Orcas Power and Light Cooperative (formed in the 1930s through the Rural Electrification Administration) brought island-wide electricity to San Juan Island (including Roche Harbor) by means of power lines in the 1950s.

McMillin established **The Company Store** to meet the needs of, as well as exploit, his employees and their families, who were paid in scrip redeemable at the store. Workers could get cash for their scrip, but there were no other merchandise outlets on the north side of the island. Nearby, along the shore and on the Pier, large warehouses stored up to 20,000 barrels of lime. On the **Pier** the Roche Harbor Fleet, consisting of three large sailing ships *(Star of Chile, William G. Irwin,* and *Archer)*, were loaded with barrels of lime for customers up and down the West Coast, and as far away as Argentina and Hawaii.

Hotel de Haro

The **Yellow Brick Road**, consisting of fire bricks taken from the abandoned lime kilns, surrounds the area near The Company Store, Pier, McMillin House, Formal Gardens, and Hotel de Haro. Double layers of these bricks, specially made from fire clay to withstand the high heat, lined the calcining chambers of the kilns. Due to wear and distortion through chemical fusion, they had to be replaced every several years. Labels stamped in the bricks indicate that many originally came from brickyards in England and Scotland, shipped out as ballast; later, fire brick was obtained from nearby British Columbia (see pages 59-60).

In order to house visiting businessmen and friends, in 1886 McMillin built the **Hotel De Haro** around an existing log structure, probably a residence for the Scurr brothers and their workers. The Hotel, designed in the Italianate Style, features balustrades and a tall, thin parapet wall that forms a "false front" to the gable roof behind.

Near the Hotel de Haro are the residences and gardens of the McMillin family. The **John S. McMillin House** was enlarged from an existing structure to create a waterfront home for his wife Louella, two sons (Fred and Paul), and daughter (Dorothy). McMillin constructed a semicircular deck, covered with a conical striped canopy, which enabled Mr. and Mrs. McMillin to overlook their garden and harbor activity. (The Tarte family added a deck and gazebo as part of its remodel into a restaurant in 1978.) Nearby, Mrs. McMillin, who may have taken her inspiration from Mrs. Butchart on the Saanich peninsula (Butchart Gardens), created the **Formal Gardens**: to the south of the walkway was the rose garden and to the north, adjacent to their residence, was the sunken garden. The **Paul McMillin House**, originally located in the northeast corner of the formal gardens, was moved to its present location in the 1920s. Paul helped with the management of Roche Harbor after the death of his brother Fred in 1922, and ran the company after the death of his father in 1936. (Fred had a house near Afterglow Beach.)

The **Chapel**, constructed in 1892 as a Methodist Church, was also used as a school. It was refurbished by the Tarte Family and consecrated as "Our Lady of Good Voyage" Catholic Church in 1960.

John and Louella McMillin

There were two areas of housing for workers at Roche Harbor: the no longer extant "Jap Town" to the south (near the present day West Point condominiums) for the Japanese employees; and one to the north, for both married and single non-Asians. About twenty **Cottages** were built around 1890, in rows all the way down to the water, to house workers with families; eight of these remain. Single working men lived in log houses and barrack-like dormitories located along the edge of the hill to the southwest. Set in the upper row of the Cottages is the **Red Schoolhouse**, which was built in the 1920s.

McMillin Family Mausoleum

To the north of the cottage area is a parking lot for visiting the **Cemetery** and **Mausoleum**. The Cemetery contains the graves of many of the company workers and other residents of Roche Harbor and its vicinity. Walking through the Cemetery and following the signs through the woods, you come to Afterglow Vista, the McMillin Family Mausoleum. John S. McMillin began work on this memorial in 1936, but died and was buried there before it was completed. Initially, the Mausoleum saw the interment of the remains of the McMillin family who had already died—John and Louella's first son, John H. (July 16, 1878), and second oldest son, Fred H. (1880-1922)—followed by John S. himself upon his death in November of 1936. Later, wife and mother Louella Hiett McMillin (1857-1943), son Paul (1886-1961), and daughter Dorothy (1894-1990) were also interred here. The structure, modeled on a seven-column circular Greek temple (*tholos*), incorporates symbols from McMillin's interest in Masonry and the Sigma Chi fraternity. For instance, the structure is approached by two sets of stairs, representing stages within the Masonic Order. The stairs on the east side of the mausoleum stand for the spiritual life of man. The winding in the path symbolizes that the future cannot be seen. The stairs were built in sets of three, five, and seven. These represent the Trinity as well as the three stages of life (youth, manhood, old age); the five orders of architecture (Tuscan, Doric, Ionic, Corinthian, Composite) and the five senses; and the seven days of Creation as well as the seven liberal arts and sciences (grammar, logic, rhetoric, arithmetic, geometry, music, astronomy). The central plan of the Mausoleum—a circular table around which chairs containing the remains of the parents and their four children were arranged—was designed to represent the gathering of the family in the hereafter. A seventh space was reserved for a "missing" chair, and its corresponding column was designed and constructed as "broken" or "incomplete," to represent the unfinished life of man on this earth. The orientation of this column was also designed so that the setting sun casts a shadow that falls between the chairs of the parents, John and Louella. This, along with the yellowish coloration of the columns, contributes to the designation of the Mausoleum as "Afterglow Vista."

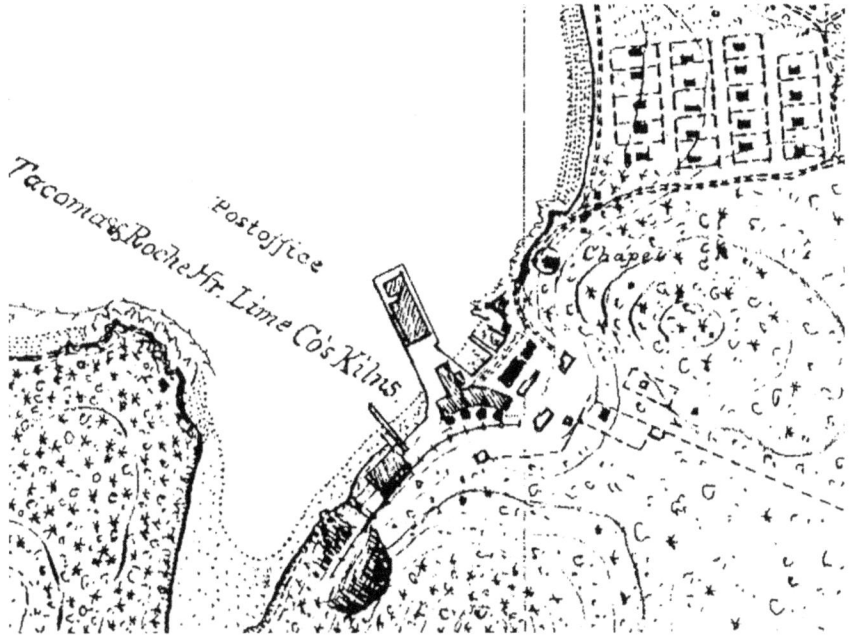

Roche Harbor, 1894

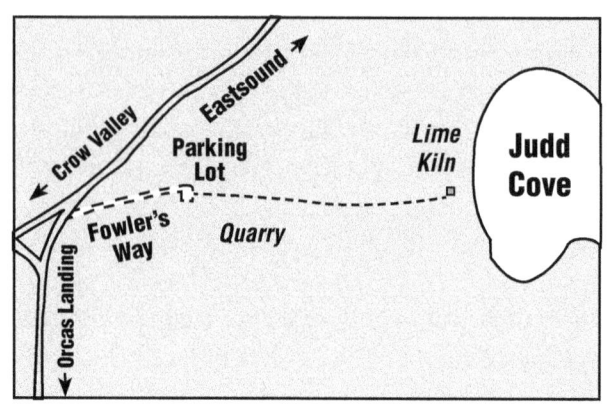

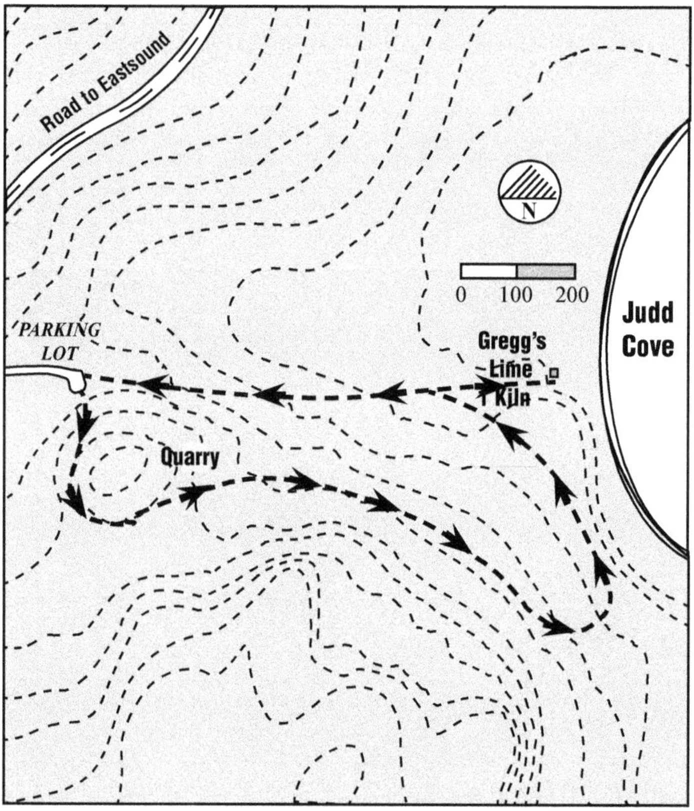

Judd Cove Quarry and Kiln
Orcas Island, Washington

TOUR GUIDE

JUDD COVE PRESERVE
McCurdy Lime Company • Gregg's Lime Kiln
Orcas Island

Judd Cove Preserve is typical of the many small lime operations in the San Juan Islands. The property was acquired by the San Juan County Land Bank in 2000 and restored with help from the Trust for Public Land, Washington State Recreation and Conservation Board, and Washington State Department of Natural Resources. In addition to tidelands, marine shoreline, and a shady conifer forest, the site is the location of a small limestone quarry and remains of a lime kiln, which was restored in 2009.

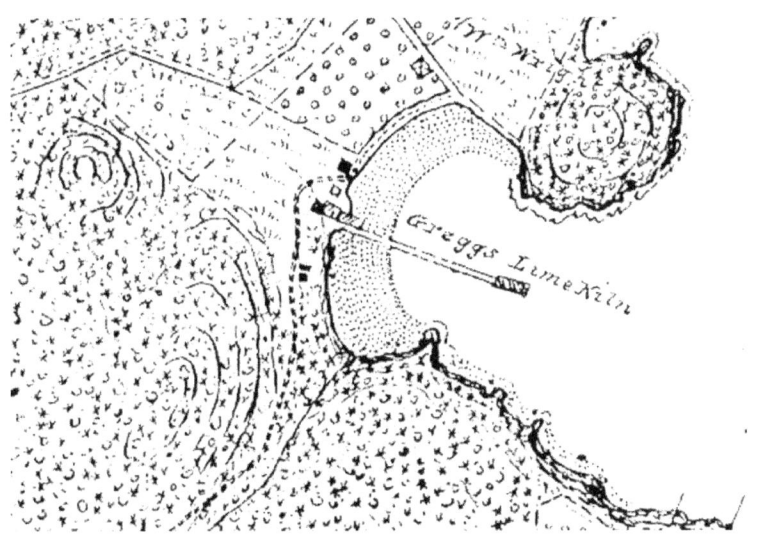

Gregg's Lime Kiln, 1889

Directions. From the Orcas ferry landing, take Orcas Road for 6.9 miles and turn right on Fowler's Way then proceed down the hill to the parking area. From Eastsound, take Orcas Road 1.1 miles and turn left onto Fowler's Way then proceed down the hill to the parking area.

Judd Cove with Gregg's Lime Kiln (lower right), Orcas Island

History. The operation at Judd Cove was one of several small lime making enterprises near Eastsound on Orcas Island. On July 8, 1888, the McCurdy Lime Company (capital stock $15,000) filed articles of incorporation with the office of Washington's Secretary of State, with directors James McCurdy (formerly of San Juan Lime Company); Nathan Gregg (Lawrence, KA); and J. C. Brittain (King County, WA). However, in September of that year, Gregg and his wife Maggie filed a suit against McCurdy and his wife Jane and Brittain and his wife Jemima. The defendants claimed to be owners of land on Orcas consisting of a "valuable deposit of lime and lime stone rock" ($2,000 worth), as well as "2 houses a partially constructed kiln for burning lime stone and also a wharf and other improvements" including "tools, lumber, fire brick, lime in barrels, provisions, materials for making barrels, quarried stone, one horse and other personal property." Apparently Gregg, who had purchased a one-third interest in the property for $666 in July of 1888, had also advanced $1,462 toward improvements and $700 for more land. On October 25, 1888, the Brittains sold Gregg the property for $2,875. Gregg then bought an additional 40 acres of land from William Wright, who had sold the original property to

McCurdy and Brittain. An 1889 U. S. Coast and Geodetic Survey map indicates "Gregg's Lime Kiln," consisting of a kiln, wharf, and several other structures on Judd Cove, but beyond that little is known about subsequent lime operations there.

Description. A half-mile loop trail provides the visitor with the opportunity to see the remains of the stone quarry and restored kiln. If you take the upland part of the trail first, you will be able to recapitulate the process whereby the limestone was quarried in small amounts from the hillside and then transported down the slope to the kiln. Near where the trail rejoins the gravel road, on a slight bluff above the kiln, workmen loaded the limestone via a trestle into the log cribbing atop the kiln. They 'burnt' the stone in the calcining chamber by feeding four-foot long pieces of firewood into the two arched fireboxes on either side of the kiln; heavy steel fire doors lined with firebricks helped keep the heat in, while ashes were removed from the arched pits below the fireboxes. At the bottom of the kiln, one can see the small arched opening where the men removed the lime—'burnt' limestone—which was placed in barrels for shipment from the wharf (demolished) nearby.

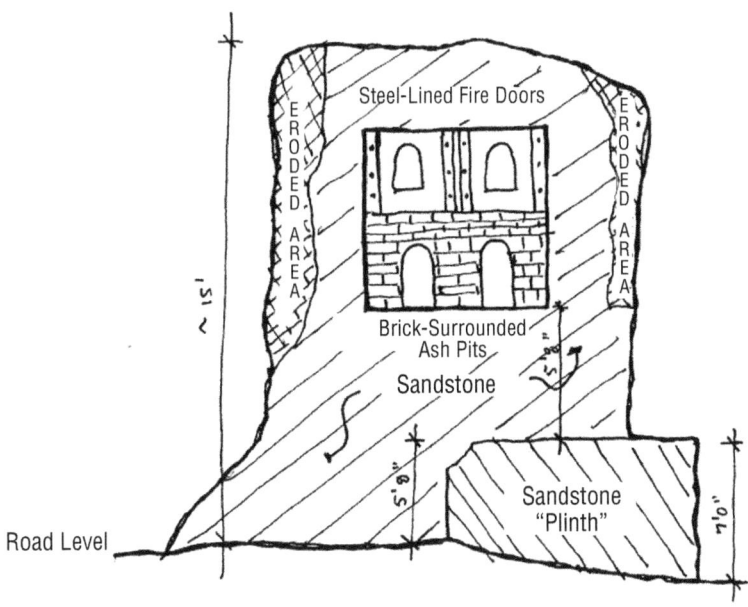

Gregg's Lime Kiln, Prior to Restoration

SUGGESTED READING

There were many sources for the material gathered in this book. For a general historical approach: Lucille S. McDonald, *Making History: The People Who Shaped the San Juan Islands* (Friday Harbor: Harbor Press, 1990); David Richardson, *Pig War Islands* (Eastsound, WA: Orcas Publishing Company, 1971); Lynette and George Bailey, *Roche Harbor: A Saga in the San Juans* (Everett: B & E Enterprises, 1972); and Richard Walker, *Roche Harbor* (Charleston, SC: Arcadia Publishing, 2009). Specific cultural historical reports include: Sharon A. Boswell and Lorelea Hudson, *Heritage Resources Investigations at the Limekiln Preserve, San Juan Island, San Juan County, Washington* (Seattle: Northwest Archaeological Associates, Inc., 2001); Boyd C. Pratt and Nancy Larsen, "San Juan Lime Company/Cowell's National Register of Historic Places Nomination Form," Washington State Department of Archaeology and Historic Preservation website; and Chris Link, *Roche Harbor Lime Kilns, San Juan County, Washington* (Seattle, WA: Northwest Archaeological Associates, Inc., July 12, 2004). For technical information on geology: Wilbert H. Danner, *Limestone Resources of Western Washington* (Olympia: Department of Conservation, 1966) and Ned Brown, *The Geology of San Juan Islands* (Bellingham: Village Books, 2014). I have done several historic structures reports for the San Juan County Land Bank—*Feature 10 Limekiln Preserve* (2004); *President Channel Preserve* (2012); and *San Juan Lime Company Boarding House* (2004)—and Roche Harbor Resorts—*Generator Plant* (2013); *Hotel de Haro* (2013); and *Lime Kiln Battery No. 2* (2010).

Primary sources include numerous local and regional newspapers published during the period, primarily the *San Juan Islander* (available online at *http://chroniclingamerica.loc.gov/lccn/sn88085190/issues*). Other early Territorial regional newspapers can be found in the Washington State digital archives: *http://www.digitalarchives.wa.gov/Home*. Several special supplements should be noted: "The San Juan Islands Illustrated Supplement," *The San*

Juan Islander 1901 and the "Supplement" to the *San Juan Islander* by the *Everett Morning Tribune* July 19, 1908. The *Friday Harbor Journal* (at the San Juan Historical Museum) is also a wealth of information. There are two articles by Wolf Bauer, "Roche Harbor During the Recovering Thirties," *The Journal of the San Juan Islands* January 8 and 15, 2003 that are especially informative. Several regional magazines featured lime works in the San Juans, particularly Roche Harbor. One in particular stands out: "One Thousand Barrels a Day," *The West Shore* August 1889. There are many cases in the Washington Territorial and State courts that involved lime kilns; these are accessible through the Washington State Archives. Of signal value are the records of *Cowell v. McMillin*, U.S. Circuit, Seattle Court Case No. 1413, Folders 1-5, Box 228, RG 21, National Archives and Records Administration, Seattle, Washington. Oral histories and other primary source material are available at the Orcas Island Historical Museum in Eastsound and the San Juan Historical Museum in Friday Harbor.

> *All this fuss has cost me labor in digesting a mass of chaff and straw in order to find a kernel of matter supposed to be contained therein. But there is no kernel.*
>
> —U. S. District Court Judge C. H. Hanford
> *Cowell v. McMillin*, Case No. 1413

A NOTE ON SPELLING

Several key words are spelled in different ways due to historic usage. East Sound refers to the body of water near Orcas Island; Eastsound is the town at the head of that body of water. Lime Kiln is a place name for the lime operations, variously know as San Juan Lime Company, McCurdy's, and Cowell's, on the west side of San Juan Island; Limekiln is the name of the San Juan County Land Bank Preserve located there.

PHOTOGRAPH AND ILLUSTRATION CREDITS

Orcas Island Historical Museum
Eastsound Lime Kiln and Dock, Orcas Island (preface)
Langdon Lime Kiln and Dock, Orcas Island (10)
Judd Cove with Gregg's Lime Kiln, Orcas Island (52)

Roche Harbor Photo Collection
Roche Harbor, San Juan Island (cover)
Stoking the Kilns, Roche Harbor, San Juan Island (17)
Barreling the Lime, Roche Harbor, San Juan Island (18)
Barreled Lime Ready to be Shipped, Roche Harbor, San Juan Island (19)
Workers' Cottages and Dormitories, Roche Harbor, San Juan Island (20)
John S. McMillin Touting His Wares (22)
Staveless Barrel Factory at Roche Harbor, San Juan Island (25)
Bagging Lime at Roche Harbor, San Juan Island (27)
Loading Lime on Ship, Roche Harbor, San Juan Island (30)
Roche Harbor, San Juan Island (31)
Roche Harbor Pit Quarry (43)
Roche Harbor Railroad Supplying Limestone to Kilns (44)
Roche Harbor Company Town & Hotel de Haro (45)
Hotel de Haro (46)
John and Louella McMillin (47)
McMillin Family Mausoleum (48)
Coopers Displaying the Tools of Their Trade, Roche Harbor (57)

San Juan Historical Museum
North Kiln and Boarding House, Lime Kiln, San Juan Island (2)
Roche Harbor during the Scurr era (9)
Hauling cordwood (14)
Lime Kiln and Quarry Crew, Cowell's, San Juan Island (21)
San Juan Lime Company (Lime Kiln) (34)
North Kiln and Boarding House (39)

Doug McCutchen
San Juan Lime Company (Lime Kiln) 2013 (34)

Township and Range Survey, General Land Office BLM
Bailey's Lime Kiln (7)
Seattle Lime Claim (10)

U. S. Coast and Geodetic Survey, Details of Puget Sound T-sheets
Langdon Lime Kiln, Orcas Island (3)
Lime Kilns in East Sound, Orcas Island (11)
Roche Harbor (49)
Gregg's Lime Kiln (51)

Maps designed by Lovel and Boyd C. Pratt; production by Bruce Conway
Diagrams, Drawings, and Graphs by Boyd C. Pratt

ACKNOWLEDGEMENTS

- Lovel Pratt, *sine qua non*
- Roche Harbor Resort, supporter of many lime-related research projects, including this book: Brent Snow, General Manager
- Nancy Larsen, co-author of National Register of Historic Places nomination for San Juan Lime Company/Cowell's—which inspired this book
- San Juan County Land Bank, custodian of many quarry and kiln sites: Lincoln Bormann, Judy Cumming, Ruthie Dougherty, Eliza Habegger, and Doug McCutchen
- San Juan Historical Museum: Kevin Loftus, Don Nixon, and Andy Zall
- Orcas Island Historical Museum: Clark McAbee, Nancy Stilger, Edrie Vinson, Jen Volmer, and Denise Wilk
- Doris Blinks, Lime Kiln researcher and enthusiast
- San Juan Island Library, research enabler: particularly Heidi Lewis, Inter Library Loan Librarian extraordinaire
- Bob Carson, Steve Cohan, Bill Engle, Cy Field, Dan Meatte, David B. Williams, and Michael E. Yeaman
- Emily Reed, editing
- W. Bruce Conway, publishing services

Coopers Displaying the Tools of Their Trade, Roche Harbor, San Juan Island

Main areas of firebrick production in Great Britain

FIREBRICKS USED IN SAN JUAN ISLANDS LIME KILNS

Manufactured from fire clay, firebricks—also called refractory bricks—were used to line the inner walls of the lime kilns, to withstand high temperatures and insulate the outer, limestone walls from the heat. At first, most firebricks were imported from England and Scotland, sometimes as ballast in ships. Later, brickyards produced firebricks in British Columbia and Washington State.

Listing: **NAME** [stamped in brick]. Company; Location; Years of operation; Type; Site in San Juans

ATLAS. Atlas Fire Brick Works; Bathgate, Scotland; ca. 1882-1973; Standard; RH

BENSON. William Benson & Son; Newcastle-on-Tyne, England; ca. 1873-1937; Standard; RH

BONNYBRIDGE. Bonnybridge Silica & Fire Clay Co., Ltd.; Bonnybridge, Stirlingshire, Scotland; ca. 1874-1971; Standard; RH

Patent BROWN & SON/PAISLEY. Robert Brown & Sons Ltd; Paisley, Renfrewshire, Scotland; ca. 1836-1938 (firebrick in 1852); Standard; JC, LK, RH

CARR. John Carr & Sons; Low Lights, Northshields, England; ca. 1844-1908; Standard; RH

T. CARR. Thomas Carr & Son; Newcastle-on-Tyne, England; ca. 1827-1918; Standard; JC, LK, RH

CLAYBURN/CANADA/[MADE IN CANADA]; Clayburn Co., Ltd; Clayburn Village, British Columbia; 1905-1931; Standard, Arch, Wedge; LK, RH

COLUMBIA X. Gladding, McBean & Co.; Washington; 1942; Standard; LK

COWEN. Joseph Cowen & Company; Blaydon-on-Tyne, England; 1823-1904; Standard; LK, RH

FOSTER. Henry Foster & Co., Ltd.; Newcastle-on-Tyne, England; ca. 1890-1963; Standard; RH

GARTCRAIG. Gartcraig Fire Clay Co., Ltd.; Gartcraig, England; ca. 1874-1967; Standard; RH

GLENBOIG. The Glenboig Union Fire Clay Co., Ltd.; Glasgow, Scotland; ca. 1882-1965; Standard; RH

HICKMAN & C/STOURBRIDGE. Hickman & Co.; Stourbridge, England; ca. 1786-1973; Standard; RH

LIVERMORE. Livermore Fire Brick Co.; California; 1942; Standard; RH

NO. 2 WED[?]. Origin unknown; Standard; RH

ROBSON. Robert and/or William Robson; Newcastle-on-Tyne, England; ca. 1863-1908; Standard; RH

RUFFORD/STOURBRIDGE. Francis T. Rufford; Stourbridge, England; 1800-1963; Standard; LK

J. H. SANKEY/CANNING TOWN.E. J[ohn]. H[art]. Sankey & Son; Canning Town, England; 1857-?; Standard; RH

SKAGIT. Not known—possibly Clayburn; Standard; RH

SNOWBALL. James and George H. Snowball; Swalwell, England, ca. 1854-1935; Standard; RH

STARWORKS/JD/GLENBOIG. The Glenboig Union Fire Clay Co., Ltd.; Glasgow, Scotland; ca. 1872-1965; Standard; RH

TYRONE. Harbison-Walker Refractories Company, PA; 1921-1942; Standard; RH

Sizes:
    Arch 2-2¾" x 4½" x 9"
    Standard 2½" x 4½" x 9"
    Wedge 2½-3½"x 4½" x 9"

Locations:
    Judd Cove (JC)
    Lime Kiln (LK)
    Roche Harbor (RH)

Sources:

John Adams, Janet Bingham, Helmi Braches, and Susanna Clemas Houwen, *Brick by Brick: The Story of Clayburn* (Clayburn, BC: Clayburn Village Community Society, 2001).

Karl Gurcke, "A Preliminary Study of San Juan Island Bricks," *San Juan Archaeology Volume II*, Roderick Sprague, ed. (Moscow, ID: University of Idaho Laboratory of Anthropology, 1983).

Karl Gurcke, *Bricks and Brickmaking: A Handbook for Historical Archaeology* (Moscow, ID: The University of Idaho Press, 1987).

LIME COMPANIES IN THE SAN JUAN ISLANDS

They are a multitude of companies that operated the limestone quarries and lime kilns in the San Juan Islands, many of them for a relatively brief time (one to five years). Most lime operations underwent changes in name and ownership; even the largest, most continuous works—at Lime Kiln and Roche Harbor—experienced this. This section attempts to record all the company names encountered in the history of limestone quarrying and limemaking in the San Juan Islands: a kaleidoscopic picture!

Bowen Brothers & Jamieson. In 1884 John G. Thompson sold his homestead on Judd Cove in East Sound, Orcas Island, to Frank H. Richards, who in turn sold it in 1888 to John Wildes Bowen of Tacoma. At the same time, Richards bonded the property to Susan Bowen, with Robert Jamieson as witness. Later that year, Susan and her husband Frank H. Bowen deeded the property to their son John Wildes Bowen. At this time the U. S. Coast and Geodetic Survey denoted a "Bowen Bros & Jamieson LK" at that site on Judd Cove. Historic photographs indicate the full works of a quarry, kiln, warehouse, and wharf at the site. Local lore has it that only one shipment of lime was produced, and that the ship carrying it sank with its cargo. In any case, the operation did not last long, for in 1891 Richards sued John W. Bowen in superior court for the note on the property. It was sold to the highest bidder, Richards himself.

Chuckanut Portland Cement Company. See ***Estelle.***

Eagle Lime Company. The Eagle Lime Company was incorporated on April 16, 1900, by Thomas Boyd, H. Harrington, and M. H. Walter, with capital comprised of 250 shares valued at $25,000. On August 23, 1900, the *San Juan Islander* reported that "The Eagle Lime Company has been organized to develop a lime ledge on the northwest shore of Orcas, about a mile from the old Wheeler kiln. The company is arranging to build a kiln of one hundred barrels daily capacity." But within a year, although the kiln had been completed, they suspended operation, "some large blasts having shown the ledge to have a surface deposit of much smaller extent and value than the owners had supposed." After another six months, the *San Juan Islander* noted that the old kiln was being torn down and a new one "with a better drought" was being constructed by some new Seattle partners. This, along with a new tramway, was finished by the end of the year, but by the next spring (April 1902), the operations had been shut down indefinitely. At the end of 1903, a sheriff's sale was held to satisfy the debts of Thomas and his wife Catharine A. Boyd to H. Harrington; a year later (December 31, 1903), the Eagle Lime Company had redeemed the property, and sold it to J. A. Soderberg. John A. and Jennie E. Soderberg in turn sold the lime properties for $10,000 to the **Orcas Lime Company** (November 17, 1904).

Estelle/Chuckanut Portland Cement Company. The narrative report of the 1888 U. S. Coast and Geodetic Survey of eastern Orcas Island noted that "At one point halfway between Point Lawrence and Racoon Bluff men were at work opening a lime stone quarry." However, *The Pacific Magazine* of April 1891 reported that "the Estelle works on the east side of Orcas, which were started two years ago, have been shut down through land office litigation." In February 1907, the property was purchased by the Chuckanut Portland Cement Company, and word was that the works would be started up again. No further information is available about this operation.

Eureka. Eureka, located north of Friday Harbor on the east coast of San Juan Island, was established around 1860 by an Englishman named Roberts. The Victoria *Colonist* noted in June of 1861 that 345 barrels of lime, the work of six men at one kiln, had been shipped from Eureka to Seattle. Roberts allegedly drowned soon thereafter. In 1879 the works were reopened by brothers Daniel and William McLachlan and their cousin by marriage, Thomas Lee. Lee bought out the McLachlan brothers in 1882 and continued to run the operations by himself; at that time there were a dozen men working for him. Eventually the operation included two kilns, a wharf, cooper's shop, cookhouse, warehouse, and blacksmith shop, in addition to workers' quarters and a store. In 1890, J. C. Werner, according to the *San Juan Graphic* "the genial superintendent of the Eureka Lime Co.," applied for a post office there, named Werner, of course. However, the operations did not last beyond the mid-1890s, for the U. S. Coast and Geodetic Survey of 1895 noted that the site was abandoned. See **Whadhams & Elliott.**

Everett Lime Company. The Everett Lime Company was incorporated by Charles C. Clauson, George J. Schuchart, Jr., and W. H. Davis at Everett in 1933, with a capitalization of $10,000. The company operated several Orcas Island quarries for paper rock, including **McGraw & Kittinger**, **Red Cross**, **Soderberg**, and West Sound, as well as the Wilson quarry on San Juan Island (they also had quarries in Bellingham and Everett). The interests of the Everett Lime Company seem to be intertwined with those of the **Mitchell Bay Lime Company**. On April 23, 1943, Clauson died in a blast accident at the Everett quarry. His son Gordon took over operations, which probably continued through the 1950s.

Gailey and Boyd. In 1889 David A. Gailey and Thomas Boyd bought land near Eastsound, Orcas Island, where they had established a quarry and lime kiln. (It appears on the U. S. Coast and Geodetic Survey of 1889 as "Dailey [sic] and Boyd's"). David and his wife Elizabeth established Gailey's First Addition to Eastsound on the property north of the county road in 1908; the quarry was in Lots 1 and 2 and the kiln on Lot A—a narrow strip of shoreline. It is not known how long the operation lasted.

Henry Cowell Lime and Cement Company. The Henry Cowell Lime and Cement Company was incorporated in Washington State on December 23, 1898. See also **San Juan Lime Company/McCurdy's/Cowell's**.

Island Lime Company. L. H. Wheeler located the "Seattle Lime Claim" on the west coast of Orcas Island on April 30, 1889. Half of the quarry lay north of the quarter section line, so at the same time his brother Lee Wheeler submitted the "Ben Harrison Lime Claim" for the southern half. Both claims were approved on April 17, 1893. Two years later, when the U. S. Coast and Geodetic Survey team mapped the western coastline of Orcas Island, they indicated an "Abandoned Lime Kiln." On February 15, 1900, the *San Juan Islander* reported the incorporation of the Island Lime Company by Alpheus Byers, Wayland B. Augir, E. M. Gordon, and J. C. Werner, all from Seattle, with capital of $1,000. A few days later Alpheus Byers filed for 20 acres of land under the Timber Land Act of 1878. In 1901, the State of Washington sued the Island Lime Company in Superior Court for trespass upon state land; after many legal maneuvers, the case was decided in March 1903 and damages of $321.75 were awarded to the state. In 1904, E. V. Cowell, representing the **Henry Cowell Lime and Cement Company**, bought the Island Lime Company for $12,000; at that time, the principal stockholders were Byers & Byers of Seattle and W. B. Augir, the manager. Cornelius Coghlan, who managed the Cowell property at Lime Kiln on San Juan Island, took over the superintendence. The Cowell management, using the "Imperial" brand, continued operations at the Island Lime works intermittently through the next few years. Limestone was still being quarried and burned there in 1913.

McCurdy Lime Company. In the late 1880s, James and Jane McCurdy, who had run lime operations (McCurdy's) on the west side of San Juan Island, began investing in land on Orcas Island near East Sound. Partnering with J. C. Brittain, of Seattle, James bought 4½ acres from William and Louise Wright on April 25, 1888. The following June, James with his wife Jane and Brittain with his wife Jemima sold the property to Nathan P. Gregg of Lawrence, Kansas, for $666.65. This constituted a third interest in the property worth $2,000 that the McCurdys and the Brittains sold on July 2nd to the McCurdy Lime Company, which had been incorporated that month, with headquarters in Eastsound and a capitalization of $15,000, by the McCurdys, Brittains, and Gregg. But by September Gregg and his wife Margaret (Maggie) had filed suit against McCurdy, Brittain, their spouses, and the Company for their investment in land with "valuable deposit of lime and lime stone rock" and "2 houses a partially constructed kiln for burning lime stone and also a wharf and other improvements" as well as barrels, tools, supplies, and other valuables. Gregg claimed that he had advanced $1,462 toward improvements and there was $700 more in other property, including, according to one witness, "tools, lumber, fire brick, lime in barrels, materials for making barrels, quarried stone, one horse and other personal properties." The Greggs asked for: the placement of the property in receivership, the dissolution of the Company, and the sale of the property to apportion their respective shares. On October 25, 1888, the Brittains sold Gregg the property for $2,875. Gregg then bought an additional 40 acres of land from William Wright, who had sold the original property to McCurdy and Brittain. An 1889 U. S. Coast and Geological Survey map indicates "Gregg's Lime Kiln," consisting of a kiln, wharf, and several other structures on Judd Cove, but beyond that little is known about subsequent lime operations there.

McCurdy's. See **San Juan Lime Company/McCurdy's/Cowell's**.

McGraw & Kittinger. In 1907, George B. Kittinger paid cash for a homestead of 160 acres near Dolphin Bay on Orcas Island; he developed this into a quarry with John H. McGraw. In 1909 McGraw & Kittinger were involved in a suit against the San Juan County Treasurer over the assessment of their property on Orcas Island, "a lime ledge near the T. C. Engleson place at Dolphin Bay." After McGraw died in 1910 the executor for his estate quit claimed his share in the property to Kittinger. It was subsequently quarried by **Westerman Lime & Rock** and the **Everett Lime Company**.

Mitchell Bay Lime Company. The Mitchell Bay Lime Company was incorporated by H. P. Troy and George F. Yantis on October 13, 1928, with Bellingham as the place of business; the capitalization was $50,000, with 50,000 shares of common stock for $1 each. The company ran several operations for paper rock in the San Juan Islands, particularly the Johnson and possibly the George E. Wilson quarries on San Juan Island, as well as the Maple Falls quarry in Whatcom County. The interests of the Mitchell Bay Lime Company seem intertwined with those of the **Everett Lime Company.**

Orcas Lime Company. The Orcas Lime Company was incorporated on October 15, 1904, by S. W. R. Dally, L. A. Norris, and A. J. Balliett, all of Seattle. Samuel William Rutter Dally and his wife Mary Louise Willets were the principal operators in the company, which was run under the management of Capt. John H. Boyce. In 1907 the Company bought adjoining land that had been homesteaded by Peter A. Peterson; they used the log house that he had built as a cook house. Dally received honorable mention at the 1909 Alaska Yukon Pacific Exposition in Seattle for "lime from the kilns at the foot of Turtleback Mountain." The Dallys had two children: Katherine Nichols and S. W. R., Jr. Katherine married Howard B. Woolston in 1922. Following her father's death in 1936, on December 28, 1937, the trustees of the Orcas Lime Company—Katherine Woolston, R. J. S. Bethell, and Arthur A. Dally—resolved to wind up the affairs of the company out of court and designated Bethell to do so. Subsequently, Katherine Woolston, "the owner of all the capital stock of the Orcas Lime Company," received its full assets. She and her husband Howard then sold most of it to Ruth A. Brown on September 24, 1940.

Port Langdon/Shotter & Company/Standard Lime Company. Port Langdon, on the east shore of Orcas Island's East Sound, was first quarried in 1862 by George R. Shotter. In 1874 it was sold to Daniel McLachlan and Robert Caines, and in the next five years over 200,000 barrels of lime were produced. By this time there were two kilns, cooper shop, warehouse and wharf, boarding house and cook house, and several other structures. *The Pacific Magazine* reported in 1891 that a Mr. Scott of Seattle purchased the property in 1882, but it failed in 1886. In the spring of 1900, the Standard Lime Company was incorporated in Seattle with Lester Turner as president, T. N. Tallentire secretary and general manager, and James Hoge, Jr., as treasurer. The company purchased the Port Langdon lime works, remodeled the existing kiln, built a new kiln, did extensive work on the tramway, and erected several new buildings.

Thomas Lee, who had worked at Eureka and Cowell's on San Juan Island, was put in charge as superintendent. By 1906, the property had changed hands again, with the product going to the Tacoma and Everett Smelters, under the ownership of R. W. Rust. Operations at Port Langdon lasted into the 1910s, but the property was abandoned by the 1920s.

Puget Sound Lime Company. The *Seattle Directory* of 1888-1890 noted that Lee and Laban Wheeler and W. T. Chalk were vice president/superintendent, secretary, and general manager, respectively, of the Puget Sound Lime Company. L. H. Wheeler located the "Seattle Lime Claim" on April 30, 1889; half of the quarry lay north of the quarter section line, so at the same time Lee Wheeler submitted the "Ben Harrison Lime Claim" for the southern half of the quarry. Both claims were approved on April 17, 1893. However, by 1895, when the U. S. Coast and Geodetic Survey team mapped the western coastline of Orcas Island, they indicated an "Abandoned Lime Kiln" in the approximate location of the current kiln remains.

Puget Sound Cement & Lime Company. The Puget Sound Cement & Lime Company was incorporated in Seattle in 1913, capitalized at $3,500,000, with the directors being Hans Pederson, Alex Polson, Austin E. Griffiths, William Thaanum, C. P. Bissett, George W. Allen, and Victor Coxhead. They purchased one thousand acres on the west side of Orcas Island and planned a large operation there to feed a 10,000-barrel-per-day cement plant in Seattle. This included crushing and screening plants with a 2,400-ton capacity per day, including two 60-ton shovels loading limestone onto a standard-gauge cars, which fed several crushers. The crushed rock would then be transported by aerial tram to barges, which would take it to Seattle. This elaborate plan was not implemented, but in 1917 John A. Soderberg and his wife Martha sold their property on the west coast of Orcas Island to the company, which did operate some quarries on Orcas.

Queen Brick & Lime Company. In 1908 the Queen Brick & Lime Company, consisting of Z. B. Rawson as president, R. L. Lusby as vice president, G. B. Lazier as treasurer, M. F. Shaw as general manager, and H. C. Applegate as secretary, purchased 260 acres of limestone land between Olga and Rosario on Orcas Island from Andrew Newhall and Francis S. Fogg. They proposed to build three kilns there to use in the manufacture of cement at Colby, Washington. Although they did erect a cook and bunk house, under the superintendency of A. Van Scheyke, the project stumbled due to a suppliers' suit for nonpayment of materials; after that was settled out of court, operations resumed in 1909. However, in 1911 Fogg and Newhall filed suit for nonpayment for the land, resulting in a sheriff's sale at the end of the year.

Red Cross. The Red Cross quarry, on the northwest side of Orcas Island, was first worked by the **Roche Harbor Lime and Cement Company** and later the **Everett Lime Company**.

Roche Harbor Lime and Cement Company. See **Tacoma and Roche Harbor Lime Company**.

San Juan Archipelago Lime Company. The San Juan Archipelago Lime Company was incorporated on December 17, 1883, in Seattle, with a capitalization of $100,000 consisting of 1,000 shares of $100 each. Among its many purposes was "building, acquiring, owning, operating, running, ... and selling limekilns" as well as other building materials and their manufacture. Despite the intriguing name of the company, no connection with lime production in the San Juans has been found.

San Juan Lime Company/McCurdy's/Cowell's. In 1860, Lyman Cutlar partnered with E. C. Gillette and Frank Newsome to produce lime on the west side of San Juan Island. Gillette sold his interest to Augustin Hibbard after the first winter of operation, and the three formed a new business—the San Juan Lime Company. Hibbard bought out Cutlar and Newsome at the end of 1864, and continued operations until the following year, when George R. Shotter and Company bought in. In 1868 Hibbard borrowed $1,500 for operations from Catherine McCurdy of Port Townsend, secured through a mortgage on the land, and bought out Shotter. A year later, he formed a partnership with Nicholas C. Bailey, Charles Huntington, and Charles Watts. This agreement was shattered three months later, when Watts murdered Hibbard. Hibbard's estate was sold in 1873 to Catherine McCurdy, who turned it over to her son, James, to operate with former San Juan Lime Company partner N. C. Bailey. The two men soon secured a contract to supply lime for the new territorial prison at Steilacoom in Puget Sound; within a few years, they had expanded production to 20,000 barrels per year. Then Bailey died, leaving his half of the company and property to his wife, Jane, and their two children. Within a few years, Jane married James McCurdy, thus uniting their ownership of the operations, then referred to as "McCurdy's." James began borrowing heavily from several sources. His mother sold her promissory note and mortgage to John S. McMillin, who then leased the property from James and Jane McCurdy for three years, beginning in September 1886. One month later, the McCurdys sold the property to Henry Cowell of San Francisco. Cowell refused to pay the mortgages on the property, forcing foreclosure by the Tacoma and Roche Harbor Lime Company; he then picked up the property at the subsequent bankruptcy sale. McMillin responded by filing suit against Cowell and others, claiming that they were depleting the resources on land leased to McMillin, but the judge found for the defendants and dismissed the case. Cowell installed one of his lime superintendents from California, Cornelius Coghlan, at the operation that was hereafter known as "Cowell's."

Seattle & Roche Harbor Lime Company. In 1899, the Seattle & Roche Harbor Lime Company was incorporated by residents of Seattle, Fairhaven, and Whatcom, with "Judge" Thomas Tallentire, who was formerly employed by the *Tacoma and Roche Harbor Lime Company* and at the time employed by the Pacific American Fisheries Company. (Tallentire was also the secretary and general manager of the *Standard Lime Company*, which worked Port Langdon beginning in 1900; he 'retired' from there to work with this company.) The company drove the piles for a 180-foot-long wharf and built an office/boarding house on 55 acres on the northern end of Henry Island, where there was an old kiln, and began producing lime in May 1900. It is not clear how long the operations lasted.

Shotter & Company. See *Port Langdon* and *San Juan Lime Company*.

Soderberg. See *Walter & Soderburg.*

Standard Lime Company. See *Port Langdon.*

Staveless Barrell Company. The "staveless barrel"—a barrel consisting of two halves—was produced by a method developed by the Waterman-Chapman Barrel Machine Company. John S. McMillin purchased rights to the process in 1891, but a fire on September 10, 1892, destroyed the plant he had built at Roche Harbor, San Juan Island. The Staveless Barrel Company was incorporated in Tacoma at the end of December 1894, and McMillin sold his rights to the company. However, principal ownership of the company remained in the family because his wife Louella held most of the stock through mortgaging some of her estate holdings. William Shultz, secretary and stockholder of the *Tacoma and Roche Harbor Lime Company*, was vice president and trustee, as well as bookkeeper, of the Staveless Barrel Company.

Stuart Island Lime Company. In 1906 there is an elusive reference in the *San Juan Islander* to a Stuart Island Lime Company: J. E. Riley was retiring as superintendent and a Mr. Smith of Seattle was taking over. It mentions H. B. Kennedy of Seattle as owning the principal stock in the company. Otherwise, little is known about this company.

Tacoma Lime Company. The Tacoma Lime Company was incorporated by C. W. Nottingham, M. B. Rankin, and C. J. Reed, at Portland, Oregon, in 1883, for "the business of manufacturing owning holding storing buying & selling both on commission and on account of the company of lime lumber cement plaster plastering hair grain feed and other articles of merchandise, manufacture, and trade." John S. McMillin stated that "the entire capital stock of said corporation [***Tacoma and Roche Harbor Lime Company***] was paid for by the purchase and transfer of all the property and assets of the Tacoma Lime Company."

Tacoma and Roche Harbor Lime Company/Roche Harbor Lime and Cement Company. In 1879, Robert and Richard Scurr bought property at Roche Harbor and, in conjunction with brothers Alexander and Donald Ross and their cousin Colin Ross, developed two kilns. John S. McMillin bought the property and works in 1886 from the Scurrs and Rosses, established the Tacoma and Roche Harbor Lime Company (incorporated December 8, 1886, by McMillin, C. P. Masterson, L. R. Manning, and T. B. Wallace, with the assets of the ***Tacoma Lime Company***), and initiated a program of improvements to the production process and physical plant. He expanded the wharfs, loading platforms, and quarries, and constructed a new cooperage, office, and warehouses. He also increased production by constructing three new kilns: one of the older stone variety and two of a newer "Monitor" design, with 'boiler steel' encasing the brick lining. By 1891, he more than doubled capacity by building Kiln Battery No. 2, a complex of eight Monitor kilns, bringing the total to thirteen kilns. Production rose from the Scurr period output of 8,000 barrels annually in the mid-1880s to almost 150,000 by the 1890s. The Roche Harbor Lime and Cement Company was incorporated on November 2, 1905, by William Shultz and Benjamin C. Clark. The purpose of the company was to provide a corporate structure for the redevelopment of the works of the Tacoma and Roche Harbor Lime Company into a Portland cement production facility. This plan was frustrated by the lawsuit bought by E. V. Cowell against John S. McMillin as well as McMillin's inability to gain investors from either Canada or the East Coast. The company continued operations until the purchase of the property by the Tarte family in the 1950s.

Wadhams & Elliott. Wadhams & Elliott was a wholesale groceries and commission merchant firm established in Portland, Oregon, in the mid-1880s by William Wadhams and Henry A. Elliott. In 1887 the firm purchased the site and works at Eureka, San Juan Island. Elliott and his wife Helen sold their interest in the property to Wadhams two years later and in the 1890 Portland Directory Wadhams & Co. lists itself as proprietors of the ***Eureka Lime Company.*** [This was probably during the period when John C. Werner was superintendent.] Wadhams and his wife Lucinda sold the property to Charles E. Ladd, another Portland resident, in 1897, after activity had ceased at Eureka.

Walter & Soderburg/Soderberg. M. H. Walter and John A. Soderberg owned land with limestone near the Eagle Lime Kiln on the west coast of Orcas Island. In 1905 they contracted with the *Pacific Coast Lime Company* to provide limestone to the "Gibson kiln" in Seattle. In early 1906, Walters sold his interest to Soderberg and moved with his family back to Seattle. Soderberg had several large bunkers and an extensive tramway, as well as bunk houses for the men working the operations, built in 1906. In 1911 he filed suit against the Pacific Portland Cement Company, the ***Orcas Lime Company***, and A. C. McRae, which the judge found for Soderberg in 1913. Four years later Soderberg and his wife Martha sold the property to the ***Puget Sound Cement & Lime Company***.

Westerman Lime & Rock. See ***McGraw & Kittinger.***

White Point. The ***Orcas Lime Company*** expanded operations to San Juan Island in 1922: Mary L. Dally purchased about 53 acres of the Scurr Ranch on White Point on San Juan Island and quit claimed the property to the Orcas Lime Company; a modern kiln was established there and operated for several years.

LIMEMAKERS IN THE SAN JUAN ISLANDS

Persons skilled in the process of making lime—burners, woodcutters, coopers, and masons—were scarce in the San Juan Islands, so they often worked at several operations. Most of the capital for limemaking in the islands came from elsewhere, principally Seattle and Tacoma. Furthermore, several of the major players in the lime industry were from places like Santa Cruz and San Francisco, California, and Victoria, B. C.

Fritz Achorn (1852-1917). Frederick "Fred" or "Fritz" G. Achorn [sometimes spelled "Acorn"] was born in 1852 in Germany. He married Augusta Julia (1852-1944) there in 1872, and they emigrated to the United States in 1882. Achorn got a homestead on Orcas (patented June 10, 1898) and farmed there for a while. He is listed as a bricklayer in the 1900 federal census and worked on masonry projects including his own fruit evaporator, some fireplaces and chimneys, and several kilns: Eagle Lime Works, Orcas, together with *James B. Fry*; kiln work at Cowell's, San Juan Island; and repair of kilns at Island Lime Company, Orcas Island. He died on September 14, 1917, and is buried in the Woodlawn Cemetery on Orcas Island.

Isaac W. Anderson (1857-1927). Isaac Wesley Anderson was born in Waverly, Pennsylvania in 1857. Anderson is listed in the 1880 census as a "lime merchant" residing in Tacoma. He was a major investor in the Tacoma and Roche Harbor Lime Company. He died in 1927 at Tacoma.

W. B. Augir (1853-1926). Wayland Bixby Augir was born in Illinois in 1853 and lived in the upper Midwest until 1890s, when he moved to Seattle. On February 15, 1900, the Island Lime Company was incorporated by *Alpheus Byers*, Augir, E. M. Gordon, and *J. C. Werner*, all from Seattle. Augir moved to Orcas and managed the company until 1904, when *Cornelius Coghlan*, who was superintendent at the Cowell property at Lime Kiln on San Juan Island, took over. Augir returned to Seattle and died at Los Angeles in 1926.

N. C. Bailey (1829-1875). Nicholas Charles Bailey was born in Cornwall, England in 1829 and married Jane Parker (1833-1935) in British Columbia in 1863; they had seven children. In 1869, he formed a partnership at Lime Kiln on San Juan Island with *Augustin Hibbard*, *Charles Huntington*, and *Charles Watts*. This agreement was shattered three months later, when Watts murdered Hibbard. Bailey was naturalized in 1873 after the boundary settlement. The property was sold in 1873 to *Catherine McCurdy* and she turned it over to her son, James, to operate with Bailey. Bailey died two years later, leaving his half of the company and property to his wife, Jane, and their two surviving children. Within a few years, Jane married *James McCurdy*, thus uniting their ownership of the operations, thence referred to as "McCurdy's."

Wolf Bauer (1912-2016). Wolf Bauer worked for the Roche Harbor Lime and Cement Company from 1936-1939. He wrote a brace of informative articles reminiscing about that time: "Roche Harbor during the Recovering Thirties," *Journal of the San Juan Islands* (January 8 and 15, 2003).

Frank H. (1825-1890) and ***John Wildes*** (1865-1943) ***Bowen***. Franklin Haylander Bowen was born in 1825 in Philadelphia, Pennsylvania. He married Susan Brown Wildes (1831-1904). In 1884 John G. Thompson sold his homestead on Judd Cove in East Sound, Orcas Island, to Frank H. Richards; Richards in turn sold it in 1888 to John Wildes Bowen of Tacoma. At the same time, Richards bonded the property to Susan, with Robert Jamieson as witness. Later that year, Frank and Susan deeded the property to their son John; at this time the U. S. Coast and Geodetic Survey denoted a "Bowen Bros & Jamieson LK" at that site. Apparently, the operation did not last long, for in 1891 Richards sued John W. Bowen in Superior Court for the note on the property. It was sold to the highest bidder, Richards himself.

Thomas Boyd (1837-?). Thomas Boyd was born in Ireland to Scots parents in March 1837. He came to the United States in 1859 and married Catharine in 1877. Boyd homesteaded land on the west coast of Orcas Island (receiving a patent in 1891), near his friend and business partner *David A. Gailey*; Gailey quitclaimed the mining rights to his land, including the "Marble Chief" and "Bald Mountain" lodes, to Boyd in 1889. In 1889 Boyd and Gailey bought land near Eastsound, where they had established a lime kiln (it appears on the U. S. Coast and Geodetic Survey of 1889 as "Dailey [sic] and Boyd's"). Boyd, along with H. Harrington, and *M. H. Walter*, incorporated the Eagle Lime Company on April 16, 1900. However, the company floundered, and was eventually the subject of a sheriff's sale in 1905.

J. C. Brittain (1835-1892). James C. Brittain was born in Pennsylvania but moved to Michigan, where he was a steamboat captain on the Great Lakes. He married Elizabeth Jordan in 1860 and they and their children moved to Seattle in 1872; he later married Jemimah M. Atkinson. Brittain worked as a steamboat captain and owner in Puget Sound, amassing a fleet of seven boats, including the *J. C. Brittain*. In 1888 he and his wife were co-owners, along with *Nathan P. Gregg* and *James and Jane McCurdy*, of the McCurdy Lime Company at Judd Cove, Orcas Island. Brittain died in California, where he was for his health, in 1892, and was buried in Seattle.

Ruth A. Brown (1894-1976). Ruth Archambault Brown was born in Detroit, Michigan, in 1894 to Charles Napoleon Brown and Malinda Archambault. She came west with a friend and worked as a director at Camp Sealth on Vashon Island, starting in 1921. In 1927 she established Four Winds Camp at Deer Harbor, Orcas Island, on property that had an old farmstead and fish cannery. She bought several lime company properties, usually through sheriff auctions, including Lime Kiln on San Juan Island and both the Eagle and Orcas Lime Kilns on Orcas Island.

Robert P. Butchart (1856-1943). Robert Pim Butchart was born in 1856 in Owen Sound, Ontario, one of eleven children. He married Jennie Foster Kennedy (1865-1943) and on their honeymoon in England learned about Portland cement. With his brother David he formed a business at Owen Sound in 1880; they were the first to put cement in sacks, rather than barrels. In 1904 he and his family moved to Tod Inlet on Vancouver Island in British Columbia and established the Vancouver Portland Cement Company (whose lime quarry became Jennie's gardens—Butchart Gardens). Butchart was good friends with *John S. McMillin*, and they would travel together on cruises on McMillin's *Calcite*. Butchart attempted to obtain Canadian and East Coast investors for McMillin's transformation of Roche Harbor into a Portland cement plant, a project that fell through. Butchart died at Victoria in 1943.

Alpheus Byers (1865-1942). Alpheus Byers was born in Pulaski, Pennsylvania, in 1865. In 1896 he married Ada Magda Christina Sjoblad and they moved to Seattle. Together with his brother Ovid, he practiced law (Byers & Byers) and invested in the Island Lime Company on Orcas Island. In 1904 he testified in the lawsuit that *E. V. Cowell* brought against *John S. McMillin*. Byers died in Seattle in 1942.

Robert Caines (1850-1927). Robert Marshall Caines was born in 1850 in New Orleans, Louisiana, the son of Captain Joseph and Mary Caines. He came round the Horn, while still an infant, to Port Townsend, where he resided until 1874 when he moved to Orcas Island. There he managed the Port Langdon quarry and kilns. He married Margaret Douglas in 1876, and they bought a place in San Juan Valley in 1883. In 1911, they moved to Saanichton, British Columbia, where he died in 1927; he is buried in the San Juan Valley Cemetery.

J. H. Cartwright J. H. Cartwright is listed as a major shareholder in the Tacoma and Roche Harbor Lime Company. Not much else is known about him.

Benjamin C. Clark (1863-1955). Benjamin Can Clark and *William Shultz* incorporated the Roche Harbor Lime and Cement Company on November 2, 1905. It is possible that he is the same person who was listed in the 1906 *Seattle City Directory* as a "secretary." In later directories and censuses, he is listed as a "timber cruiser" and broker of timber land.

Charles C. Clauson (1884-1943). Charles Cornelius Clauson was born at Forest City, Iowa, in 1884. He married Mary E. Johnson (1876-1958) there in 1908 and they had two children, Charles Gordon (1910-1991) and Mary Elizabeth (1916-1939). By 1910 they had moved to Whatcom. Clauson was involved in both the Mitchell Bay Lime Company (incorporated 1928) and the Everett Lime Company (incorporated at Bellingham in 1933), with interests in quarries on both Orcas and San Juan Islands, as well as Maple Falls (Whatcom County) and Granite Falls (Snohomish County). He died in an explosion at his quarry at Granite Falls in 1943. His son Gordon took over the operations of the Everett Lime Company, which quarried paper rock in the San Juans into the 1950s.

Cornelius Coghlan (1851-1925). Cornelius Coghlan was born in County Cork, Ireland and emigrated to the United States in 1874. In 1883 he married Catherine R. Zimmerman (1861-?) in California. He moved to San Juan Island in 1896 and assumed superintendency of Cowell's (formerly McCurdy's) Lime Kiln. When *E. V. Cowell* purchased the Island Lime Company on Orcas Island in 1904, Coghlan took over management from *W. B. Augir*. He died September 11, 1925, at Friday Harbor.

Henry (1819-1903) and ***E. V. (Ernest Victor)*** (1859-1911) ***Cowell***. Born in Massachusetts, Henry Cowell arrived at San Francisco in 1849 during the height of the California Gold Rush. He first captured the drayage and storage market, and then in 1865, along with *Isaac Davis*, bought the half interest in Jordan and Davis, a lime manufacturing concern in Santa Cruz, from *Albion Paris Jordan*. Cowell moved there to supervise the new firm of Davis & Cowell. Upon the retirement of Davis, Cowell acquired his share, thus becoming the sole owner of the largest lime manufacturing empire (the Cowell Lime & Cement Company) in California, and therefore the West Coast. In order to get a foothold in the Pacific Northwest, he bought shares in the Tacoma & Roche Harbor Lime Company in the late 1880s as well as Lime Kiln, on the west coast of San Juan Island, from *James and Jane McCurdy* in 1886. From this stemmed the great rivalry between Cowell and *John S. McMillin*. Henry Cowell was shot to death on the streets of San Francisco in 1903. His son, E. V. Cowell, took over the business and launched a lawsuit against McMillin in 1906, in part to delay McMillin's efforts to turn Roche Harbor into a Portland cement factory. E. V. built the town and factory of Cowell in California, completed 1908, just before the lawsuit ended. He continued to manage his San Juan (Cowell's) and Orcas (Imperial or Island Lime Company) until his death in 1911.

Lyman Cutlar (1852?-1874). Possibly born in Kentucky, Lyman Cutlar was involved in the gold rush in British Columbia in 1858. A year later he had moved to San Juan Island and, squatting on Hudson's Bay Company pastureland, shot a company pig, which touched off the Pig War controversy. Cutlar partnered with *E. C. Gillette* and *Frank Newsome* in 1860 to produce lime at what would become the San Juan Lime Company on the west side of San Juan Island. He was out of the business in a few years and disappeared from the island, reappearing in Skagit County in 1871 and dying in the Bellingham area in 1874.

S. W. R. Dally (1860-1936). Samuel William Rutter Dally and his wife Mary Louise Willets (1862-1928) were the principal operators in the Orcas Lime Company, which was run under the management of Capt. John H. Boyce. In 1907 the Company bought adjoining land that had been homesteaded by Peter A. Peterson; they used the log house that he had built as a cook house. Dally received honorable mention at the 1909 Alaska Yukon Pacific Exposition in Seattle for lime. In 1922, Mary L. Dally purchased about 53 acres of the Scurr Ranch on White Point on San Juan Island and quit claimed the property to the Orcas Lime Company; a modern kiln was established there. The Dallys had two children: Katherine Nichols and S. W. R., Jr. Katherine (1901-1971) married Howard B. Woolston in 1922. Upon her father's death in 1936, the trustees of the Orcas Lime Company resolved to wind up the affairs of the company and Katherine Woolston received its full assets. She and her husband Howard then sold most of it to *Ruth A. Brown* on September 24, 1940.

Wilbert R. Danner (1924-2012). Wilbert Roosevelt "Ted" Danner was born and educated in Washington State and became a professor of geology at the University of British Columbia in 1954. Danner surveyed kiln and quarry sites in San Juan County for his *Limestone Resources of Western Washington* (1966). Danner, known for collecting bottles and cans to raise funds for university students, established the Beer-Pop Can-Bottle Deposit Refund Award and donated over a million dollars to the University upon his death in 2012.

Isaac Davis (1845-1911). Isaac Ely Davis was born in Dubuque, Iowa, in 1845. As a child he moved with his family to California, and started the firm of Jordan and Davis, a lime manufacturing concern in Santa Cruz, with *Albion Paris Jordan*. In 1865 Henry Cowell, bought Jordan's half interest; in 1888, he acquired Davis's share, thus becoming the sole owner of the largest lime manufacturing empire in California. Davis married Mary Elizabeth Sophia Horton (1856-1939) in 1875 and they had eight children. He died in 1911 and is buried in Watsonville, California.

Francis S. Fogg (1848-1929). Francis Sumner Fogg was born in 1848 in Boston, Massachusetts. He married Emma F. Heath (1848-?) in 1874. By the 1900 census, Fogg was on Orcas Island, working as a millwright—presumably for Andrew Newhall. In 1902 Fogg worked with *Thomas H. Lee* on the Standard Lime Company's operations at Port Langdon. Newhall convinced him to homestead land between Rosario and Olga that contained limestone, and Fogg got a patent for 152 acres, which he sold, along with some land of Newhall's, to the Queen Brick and Lime Company in 1908. However, the project did not last, and Fogg and Newhall were obliged to sue the company for lack of payment. The property was sold at sheriff's auction in late 1911. Fogg died at Friday Harbor in 1929.

James B. Fry (1865-1935). James Bird Fry was born in 1865 in New York State to John N. Fry and Sarah Jane Scoffield, both of whom were from Holland. John Fry moved his family first to Iowa and then Orcas Island in 1879. Although he is listed as a mason in the 1880 federal census, he also farmed. His son James B. Fry is listed as a plasterer in the 1900 federal census and built and repaired several lime kilns in the islands. He married Mary Emma Smith (1874-1965) in 1889 in Seattle and they had six children. His works include: a kiln on Henry Island; Eagle Lime

Works (Orcas), together with *Fritz Achorn*; overhaul of kilns at Cowell's (San Juan Island); Island Lime Company (Orcas Island); repair of kilns at Roche Harbor (San Juan Island); and rebuilding Port Langdon kiln (Orcas Island) with F. G. Head. In 1908 James moved with his family to Texada Island, British Columbia, where he built four kilns and other improvements. He died in 1935 at Seattle.

David A. Gailey (1862-1954). David Andrew Gailey was born in Illinois in 1862 and he moved to Seattle right after the fire of 1889. He married Elizabeth Steel (1869-1976) in Philadelphia, Pennsylvania, in 1893. Gailey homesteaded land on the west coast of Orcas Island (receiving a patent in 1891), near his friend and business partner *Thomas Boyd*; Gailey quitclaimed the mining rights to his land, including the "Marble Chief" and "Bald Mountain" lodes, to Boyd, in 1889. In the same year, Boyd and Gailey bought land near Eastsound from L. Sutherland, where they established an upland quarry and a shoreline kiln. David and Elizabeth established Gailey's First Addition to Eastsound on the property north of the county road in 1908; the quarry was in Lots 1 and 2 and the kiln on Lot A—a narrow strip of shoreline. He died at Seattle in 1954.

J. J. Gilbert (1845-1929). John J. Gilbert supervised the U. S. Coast and Geodetic Survey of the San Juan Islands during the 1880s and 1890s. Both in the descriptive reports and on the T (Topographic) Sheets Gilbert noted the presence of lime kilns and quarries throughout the islands, sometimes including extensive commentary on the works during that period.

E. C. Gillette (1823-1905?). Edward C. Gillette was born in Massachusetts about 1823. Along with *Lyman Cutlar* and *Frank Newsome*, he was one of the founders of the operations at Lime Kiln on San Juan Island in 1860. Before that, he may have been the surveyor mentioned by Belle Vue Sheep Farm Chief Trader Charles Griffin and the Northwest Boundary Survey team as platting parcels for preemption in San Juan Valley. Gillette is listed as a mining engineer and surveyor in the 1860s and 1870s in the mining districts of British Columbia and was appointed in 1874, and then subsequently elected San Juan County Surveyor. In the 1890s he bought and sold land on Decatur Island. Based on legal notices, he appears to have died around 1905.

Nathan P. Gregg (1840-1908). Captain Nathan Preston Gregg, who was born in Ohio, married Margaret Duncan (1847-1908) in 1868 after fighting in the Civil War. They bought property from *J. C. and Jemimah Brit-*

tain and *James and Jane McCurdy* for a lime kiln at Judd Cove (McCurdy Lime Company) but sued them for not providing their share of the investment. It only lasted a few years, as Gregg is listed as a farmer in the 1900 census and their household included a farm hand. Gregg died on March 5, 1908, and is buried at the Woodlawn Cemetery in Eastsound.

C. H. Hanford (1849-1926). Judge Cornelius Holgate Hanford was born in Iowa and nominated by President Benjamin Harrison to the United States District Court for the District of Washington in Seattle. He presided over *Cowell v. McMillin*, Case No. 1413 (1906-1909), finally concluding that "All this fuss has cost me labor in digesting a mass of chaff and straw in order to find a kernel of matter supposed to be contained therein. But there is no kernel." Hanford was the subject of a House of Representatives impeachment inquiry and resigned his position during the proceedings; he returned to private practice and died at Seattle in 1926.

Augustin Hibbard (1829-1869). In 1861, *E. C. Gillette* sold his interest in the lime kiln that he had started with *Lyman Cutlar* and *Frank Newcombe* to Augustin Hibbard, and the three formed a new business—the San Juan Lime Company. Hibbard bought out Cutlar and Newsome at the end of 1864, and continued operations until the following year, when *George R. Shotter* and Company bought in. In 1868 Hibbard borrowed $1,500 for operations from *Catherine McCurdy* of Port Townsend, secured through a mortgage on the land, and bought out Shotter. A year later, he formed a partnership with *Nicholas C. Bailey*, *Charles Huntington*, and *Charles Watts*. This agreement was shattered three months later, when Watts murdered Hibbard.

Charles Huntington. Little is known about this Canadian partner of *Nicholas C. Bailey* and *Charles Watts*.

Lee Ingram (1835-1899). Leander Ingraham was born in 1835 at Augusta, Maine. He married Electra Arominta Meservy (1844-1907) in Port Townsend in 1875. Ingram worked as a cooper at McCurdy's (Lime Kiln) on San Juan Island and is named, along with *Henry Cowell*, *Lloyd Tevis*, and *Richard and Robert Scurr* in an 1889 lawsuit by *John S. McMillin*. Ingram died on San Juan Island in 1899.

Robert Jamieson. In 1884 John G. Thompson sold his homestead on Judd Cove in East Sound, Orcas Island, to Frank H. Richards, who in turn sold it in 1888 to *John Wildes Bowen* of Tacoma. At the same time,

Richards bonded the property to *Susan Bowen*, with Robert Jamieson as witness. Later that year, Frank H. Bowen and his wife Susan deeded the property to their son John Wildes Bowen. At this time the U. S. Coast and Geodetic Survey included a "Bowen Bros & Jamieson LK" at that site. Nothing else is known about Robert Jamieson.

J. M. Keen (1861-1927). At first in the Tacoma real estate business with *C. P. Masterson*, and *L. R. Manning*, John M. Keen was an early investor and officer of the Tacoma and Roche Harbor Lime Company as well as the Staveless Barrell Company.

W. W. Kirkwood (1867-1900). Wallace W. Kirkwood was born in Iowa in 1867 and came to Seattle in the mid-1880s. He was one of the initial stockholders of the Tacoma and Roche Harbor Lime Company. He died in King County, Washington, in 1900.

George B. Kittinger (1865-1933). George Batchelder Kittinger was born in Flemington, New Jersey, and came to Seattle, where he married Mary Carroll Terry in 1887. In 1907, Kittinger paid cash for a homestead of 160 acres near Dolphin Bay on Orcas Island; he developed this into a quarry with *John H. McGraw*. After McGraw died in 1910 the executor for his estate quit claimed his share in the property to Kittinger.

Thomas H. Lee (1829-1910). Thomas Humphrey Lee was born in County Cork, Ireland. In 1855 he married Margaret Kirkwood (1832-1903) and they had nine children. Around 1879 he operated the Eureka (San Juan Island) quarries and kilns with his relatives by marriage, *Daniel and William McLachlan*. They would later work at Port Langdon, and Lee worked for a time at McCurdy's/Cowell's. (In 1889, James Lee (1801-1890), who had moved to San Juan to be with his son Thomas, brought a case of grand larceny against three men at the Eureka Lime Kiln.) Thomas H. Lee moved to Vancouver, British Columbia, in the 1888 and worked at the lime works on Texada Island for about a dozen years. In 1901 he was back at the Port Langdon Lime works, where he superintended the works for the Standard Lime Company. Lee died at New Westminster, British Columbia, in 1910.

L. R. Manning (1856-1924). Lucius R. Manning was born in Oswego, New York, in 1856. He learned the business of banking and came to Tacoma in 1885, where he established the Pacific National Bank of Tacoma, together with *Charles P. Masterson*, *T. B. Wallace*, W. D. Tyler, and James P. Stewart. He helped *John S. McMillin* establish the Tacoma and Roche

Harbor Lime Company, where he served as secretary, stockholder, and trustee. Masterson married Lucy Bass (1868-1914) in 1888 and they had one son. He died in 1924 at Tacoma.

Thomas Maskey (1804-1871). After the murder of *Augustin Hibbard* in 1869, Thomas Maskey came from the East Coast with his wife Sophia, one of the three heirs to Hibbard's estate. However, Maskey himself died in 1871 and was buried in Victoria, British Columbia. Despite Sophia's efforts to claim the estate, it was put up for public auction for the mortgage debt of *Catherine McCurdy*, who bought it back herself.

Charles P. Masterson (1853-1905). Charles Parker Masterson was born in Danby, New York, in 1853. A lawyer by training, he moved to Tacoma in 1885 and together with *L. R. Manning, T. B. Wallace*, W. D. Tyler, and James P. Stewart organized the Pacific National Bank of Tacoma. He helped *John S. McMillin* established the Tacoma and Roche Harbor Lime Company as a stockholder and trustee. He died in 1905 at Seattle.

Catherine (1814-1892) and ***James*** (1840-1897) ***McCurdy***. Catherine Boyd was born in 1814 in Ireland and married Samuel McCurdy (1805-1865) in 1839 in New Brunswick, Canada. James, their first son, was born there in 1840. The McCurdys moved to Port Townsend in 1860, where Samuel was surgeon at the United States Marine Hospital, but he died at sea in 1865. Catherine remained there until 1879, when she moved to San Francisco. She invested in several enterprises in the region, including the McCurdy Block on Water Street in Port Townsend and the San Juan Lime Company at Lime Kiln on San Juan Island. After her purchase of the latter property in 1873, she established her son James, who married Jane Parker (1833-1935), the widow of recently deceased partner *N. C. Bailey*. James ran McCurdys Lime Kiln until he sold it in 1886 to *Henry Cowell*. He and Jane, in partnership with *J. C. and Jemima Brittain* and *Nathan P. Gregg*, invested in the McCurdy Lime Company on Orcas, but this failed within a year, and James returned with his family to Port Townsend. Catherine died in San Francisco in 1892, and James died at Port Townsend in 1897.

John H. McGraw (1850-1910). John Harte McGraw was born in Bancroft, Maine, and married May Lizzie Kelley (1852-1907) there in 1874. They came to Seattle in the late 1870s. McGraw partnered with *George B. Kittinger* in developing a lime quarry near Dolphin Bay on Orcas Island around 1907. After McGraw died in 1910 the executor for his estate quit claimed his share in the property to Kittinger.

William (1842-1905), *Daniel* (1844-1916), and *Robert* (1848-1907) *McLachlan*. The McLachlan brothers were born in Ontario, Canada: William in 1842, Daniel in 1844, and Robert in 1848. In 1863 Daniel came to Orcas Island, where he joined with *George R. Shotter* to begin the lime works at Port Langdon on the east shore of East Sound. In 1865 he and Shotter operated the works at Lime Kiln on San Juan Island. Shotter & Company went back to Orcas and operated there at least until 1870. After Shotter's departure, Daniel ran Port Langdon with *Robert Caines*. Daniel and William McLachlan later owned and operated Eureka on the northeast coast of San Juan Island with their cousin by marriage, *Thomas Lee*. William, who moved to Seattle in the early 1880s, died there in 1905. Robert, who lived in Deer Harbor, Orcas Island, died there in 1907. Daniel died in 1916 at Victoria, British Columbia.

John S. (1855-1936) *and Paul* (1886-1962) *McMillin*. John Stafford McMillin grew up in limestone-rich Indiana. In 1882 he moved to Tacoma, where he was first involved with lime in the Puyallup Valley. In 1886, he incorporated the Tacoma and Roche Harbor Lime Company, bought the lime works at Roche Harbor from the Rosses and Scurrs, and built the operations into the largest lime works on the West Coast. McMillin married Louella Hiett (1857-1943) in 1877 and they had four children. After his elder brother Fred (1880-1922) died, Paul Hiett McMillin took over as vice president and then assumed the presidency in 1936, after his father died. All the family members were interred in the McMillin Mausoleum at Afterglow. John S. McMillin's chair/crypt reads "A 32° MASON, KNIGHT TEMPLAR, Σ X, METHODIST, REPUBLICAN, OCT 28 1855 – NOV 3 1936."

Shigeru Nagaoka (1906-1994). Shigeru "Bill" Nagaoka was born at Roche Harbor, San Juan Island, where his father Sukeichi "Jim" Nagaoka was the chief steward for the McMillin family. There was an extensive Japanese settlement at Roche Harbor, where they worked as cooks, stewards, and quarrymen.

Frank Newsome (1831-?). Born in 1831 in Virginia, Frank Newsome (Newsom) worked with *Lyman* Cutlar and *E. C. Gillette* as a lime burner at the San Juan Lime Company at Lime Kiln on the west coast of San Juan Island. It is not known what happened to him after he left in 1861.

Charles W. Nottingham (1848-1931). Charles Wesley Nottingham was born in Sangamon, Illinois, in 1848. He moved to Portland, Oregon in 1883. Along with M. B. Rankin and C. J. Reed, Nottingham was an incorporator of the Tacoma Lime Company in 1883. Based in Portland, Oregon, he worked as a broker of lime, cement, and plaster, and filed an affidavit in the lawsuit *Cowell v. McMillin*. Nottingham married Georgiana E. Pallett (1851-1934) and they had five children. He died in 1931 at Portland.

T. T. Paxson (1862-1940). Thomas Thorne Paxson was born in 1862 in Ohio. He married Lovina (1871-?) in 1888. T. T. Paxson arrived in San Juan County ca. 1890. He worked at the Island Lime Company on Orcas Island and assumed the superintendency when *W. B. Augir* was away, eventually taking over in 1904. He was involved in the limestone industry until 1907 and then ranched. In 1916, Paxson moved to Friday Harbor and, along with William McCrary, founded the Friday Harbor Brick and Tile Company in 1921, which produced concrete blocks for buildings in Friday Harbor and elsewhere on San Juan Island. He died in 1940 at Friday Harbor and his gravesite in the Valley Cemetery is bordered by concrete blocks.

Alexander (1824-1903), ***Colin*** (1826-1910), and ***Donald*** (1841-1924) ***Ross***. Alexander Ross was born in Nova Scotia, Canada, in 1824 and emigrated to the United States in 1851; Donald Ross was also born in Nova Scotia and emigrated in 1861. Their cousin, Colin Ross, was born in Scotland in 1826 and was naturalized at Port Townsend in 1877. In 1882 Alexander and Donald became partners with the *Scurr* brothers in the initial development of the lime works at Roche Harbor; Colin joined them in 1884. *John S. McMillin* bought them all out in 1886. They became ranchers and farmers in San Juan Valley.

Richard (1831-1909) and ***Robert*** (1834-1913) ***Scurr***. Richard and Robert Frederick Scurr were born in England and came to the United States in 1850, eventually moving to California. Robert came to San Juan Island in 1870 and worked as a foreman at the San Juan Lime Company/McCurdy's until 1881, when he and his brother established the lime works at Roche Harbor. In 1886 they sold their operation to *John S. McMillin*, who formed the Tacoma and Roche Harbor Lime Company. They then bought farmland on White Point. Richard died in 1909, and Robert married Annetta (Nettie) Hill (1866-1935). He died in 1913 and Nettie continued to farm on their place.

George R. Shotter (1838-1915). George R. Shotter was born in Sussex, England, in 1838 and emigrated to the United States in the early 1860s. In Victoria, British Columbia, he met up with *Daniel McLachlan* and they quarried Port Langdon, on the east shore of Orcas' East Sound, in 1863. In 1865 he and McLachlan bought in to the operation at Lime Kiln on San Juan Island. *Augustin Hibbard* bought Shotter out in 1868. Shotter & Company went back to Orcas and operated there at least until 1870, when the census recorded their works there. In the late 1860s he married Lucy Cunningham (1851-1893) and they had several children. After the boundary settlement Shotter and his family moved to Victoria, British Columbia, and they stayed in Canada until around 1893, when he moved to Alaska to superintend the Treadwell gold mine in Douglas. He died there in 1915.

William Shultz (1861-1925). William Shultz was born in 1861 at Delphi, Indiana. In 1889 he moved to Tacoma, and a year later to Roche Harbor, San Juan Island, where he started as bookkeeper and eventually became general manager, superintendent, and ultimately vice-president of the Tacoma and Roche Harbor Lime Company, as well as vice-president of the Staveless Barrel Company. After leaving the company in 1905, he went into the fishing and canning industry. He died at Friday Harbor in 1925.

J. A. Soderberg (1862-1935). Johan Albin Söderberg was born in Sweden in 1862. He emigrated to the United States in 1882 and petitioned for naturalization in 1894. Enumerated as John Soderberg in the 1900 census, his occupation is listed as a stonecutter. He married Jennie E. (?-1905) and later Martha Anderson (1879-1963) in 1907; he and Martha had five children. John and Jennie sold some limestone land on the west coast of Orcas Island to the Orcas Lime Company in 1904. Soderberg partnered with *M. H. Walter*, a builder by trade, in 1905, but a year later Walter transferred his interest in the property for $10,000. John and Martha sold the property to the Puget Sound Cement & Lime Company in 1917. John Soderberg died at Seattle in 1935.

Thomas Tallentire (1875-1945). Thomas Norbert Tallentire was born at Olympia, Washington, in 1875 and married Mary Jane Sandwith (1877-1954) in 1900 at Seattle. In 1899, the Seattle & Roche Harbor Lime Company was incorporated by residents of Seattle, Fairhaven, and Whatcom, with "Judge" Thomas Tallentire, who was formerly employed by the Roche Harbor Lime Company and was at the time employed by the Pacific American Fisheries Company. (Tallentire was also the secretary and general manager of the Standard Lime Company, which worked Port Langdon beginning in 1900; he 'retired' from there to work with this company.) He died at Los Angeles in 1945.

Lloyd Tevis (1824-1899). Lloyd Tevis was born in 1824 at Shelbyville, Kentucky. In 1850 he was living in Sacramento, California, where he married Susan Gano Sanders in 1854. In the census he is listed as a capitalist and a broker; he was partners with *Henry Cowell* when Cowell bought the McCurdys' property at Lime Kiln on San Juan Island in 1886. Cowell refused to pay the mortgage, forcing it into receivership, and then promptly bought the property for less cost at the sheriff's sale. Tevis died at San Francisco in 1899.

A. D. Tift (1851-1926). Albertus (Adelbert) Degras Tift was born in Clayton, New York, in 1851. He came out west in the late 1880s and married Elizabeth B. Connors (1861-1949) in 1890 and they resided on Shaw Island, along with his father (W. D.), mother, brother, and sister. Tift ran operations at the Lutz quarry on Shaw Island and Cliff Island; the Everett Smelter Company produced lime rock for their smelter in the mid-1890s. He died at Friday Harbor in 1926.

Ed Tuck (1911-2009). Edward Norman Tuck was born on San Juan Island; in 1932 he married Angela Sarah Kreger (1914-1991), who was born at Rocher Harbor. Ed Tuck worked most of the jobs at Roche Harbor, including quarrying, rock crushing, firing the kilns, running the power plant, and foreman.

James Tulloch (1848–1936). James Francis Tulloch came to Orcas Island in the 1870s and married Nancy Anne "Annie" Brown (1856–1941) in 1876. He homesteaded, receiving a patent in 1907, and farmed and hired out as an orchardist, but to get established he first worked at Port Langdon cutting wood and feeding the kilns. He died on Orcas Island in 1936.

Wa Chung (1844-?). Wa Chung is enumerated in the 1880 census as a 36-year-old Chinese cook at the McCurdy Lime Company on the west side of San Juan Island.

William Wadhams (1831-1905). William Wadhams was born at Wadhams Mills, New York, in 1831, and married Lucinda Agnela Skinner there in 1854; they had two children. In the mid-1860s they moved to Portland, Oregon, where he set up as a wholesale grocer and commission merchant, forming the firm of Wadhams and Elliott, together with Herny A. Elliot (1837-1903), in the mid-1880s. In 1887 the firm purchased the site and works at Eureka, San Juan Island. Elliott and his wife Helen sold their interest in the property to Wadhams two years later and in the 1890 *Portland Directory* Wadhams & Co. lists itself as proprietors of the Eureka Lime Company. [This was probably during the period when *John C. Werner* was superintendent.] Wadhams and his wife Lucinda sold the property to Charles E. Ladd, another Portland resident, in 1897, after activity had ceased at Eureka.

Thomas B. Wallace (1858-?). Thomas Bates Wallace was born in Lexington, Missouri, in 1858. An engineer by training and working with the United States Engineering Corps, he came to Tacoma in 1882 and three years later helped establish the Pacific National Bank of Tacoma, together with *L. R. Manning*, *Charles P. Masterson*, W. D. Tyler, and James P. Stewart. (He was also one of the incorporators of the Fidelity Trust Company of Tacoma in 1889.) He helped *John S. McMillin* establish the Tacoma and Roche Harbor Lime Company as stockholder and trustee. Wallace married Elizabeth Shelby Darnall in 1896 and they had three children. He died at Tacoma in 1910.

M. H. Walter (1864-1942). Malcom Hugh Walter was born in Ontario, Canada, in 1864 and emigrated to the United States in 1887. In 1891 he married Lotta May Brown (1868-1964). A builder by trade, Walter, along with *Thomas Boyd* and H. Harrington, incorporated the Eagle Lime Company on April 16, 1900. After the sheriff's sale of the company in 1905, he partnered with *John A. Soderberg* on working limestone land on the west coast of Orcas Island, but a year later he transferred his interest in the property to Soderberg for $10,000 and moved back to Seattle with his family. He died at Long Beach, California, in 1942.

Charles Watts (1831-?). On June 17, 1869, Charles Watts murdered his San Juan Lime Company partner *Augustin Hibbard* at the company office. The subsequent trial went through several lengthy jurisdictional venues due to the uncertain status of the "Disputed Islands," as the San Juans were then called, eventually ending up with an appeal to the U. S. Supreme Court. Seven years later, after the Supreme Court upheld the guilty verdict, Watts managed to escape his prison keepers—and his hanging—and was never seen or heard from again.

J. C. Werner (1864-1951) In 1890, John C. Werner, according to the *San Juan Graphic* "the genial superintendent of the Eureka Lime Co." applied for a post office there, named Werner, of course. However, the operations did not last until the mid-1890s (the post office closed in 1892), for the U. S. Coast and Geodetic Survey of 1895 noted that the site was abandoned. In 1896, Werner and his wife Alice moved to Anacortes and eventually to South Seattle.

Lee (1854-1936) and ***L. H.*** (1857-1952) ***Wheeler***. Albert Lee Wheeler was born in Wisconsin in 1854; his brother Laban Homer was born there in 1859. The *Seattle Directory* of 1888-1890 noted that Lee and Laban Wheeler and W. T. Chalk were vice president/superintendent, secretary, and general manager, respectively, of the Puget Sound Lime Company. L. H. Wheeler located the "Seattle Lime Claim" on April 30, 1889 on the west coast of Orcas Island; half of the quarry lay north of the quarter section line, so at the same time Lee Wheeler submitted the "Ben Harrison Lime Claim" for the southern half of the quarry. Both claims were approved on April 17, 1893. Lee later testified in *State of Washington vs. Island Lime Company* (1903) that the operations only ran for a year or so. Lee died in Seattle in 1936; Laban, who worked as an attorney and was a Washington State senator, died in Santa Rosa, California, in 1952.

Wing Ha (1840-?). Wing Ha is listed as a 30-year-old Chinese cook at the San Juan Lime Company on San Juan Island in the 1870 census.

INDEX

A

Achorn, Fritz, 71, 77
American Smelting and Refining Company (ASARCO), 13
Anderson, Isaac W., 71
Archer, 18, 45
Augir, W. B., 63, 71, 74, 82
Austrians, 20

B

Bailey, N. C., 5, 67, 71-72, 80
Bauer, Wolf, 72
Bellingham, 12, 14, 54, 63, 65, 74–75
Bowen, 61, 72, 79
Bowen Brothers & Jamieson, 10, 61
Boyd, Thomas, 61, 63, 72, 77, 85
Brittain, J. C., 10, 52, 64, 73
Brown, Ruth A., 65, 73, 76
Butchart, Robert P., 27, 73
Byers, Alpheus, 63, 71, 73

C

Caines, Robert, 65, 74, 81
calcium carbonate, 1
California, 3, 9, 12, 23, 28, 60, 68, 71, 73–76, 83–86
Cartwright, J. H., 74
Chuckanut Portland Cement Company, 61–62
Clark, Benjamin C., 69, 74

Clauson, Charles C., 62-63, 74
Coghlan, Cornelius, 63, 68, 71, 74
cooperage, 17, 32, 35–36, 41, 69
cordwood, 14–15, 17
Cowell, E. V., 22, 28, 63, 69, 73–75
Cowell, Henry, 9, 22–23, 33, 63, 68, 74–76, 79, 80, 84
crib, 17
Cutlar, Lyman, 3, 33, 67, 75, 77–78, 81

D

Dally, S. W. R., 65, 75
Danner, Wilbert R., 1, 31, 76
Davis, Isaac, 23, 76
Deadman Bay, 1–2, 33
Douglas fir, 15

E

Eagle Lime Company, 10, 61–62, 72, 85
Estelle, 61–62
Eureka, 3-4, 21, 62, 66, 70, 79, 81, 84–85
Everett, 12–13, 30, 62–63, 65–67, 74, 84
Everett Lime Company, 62, 65, 67, 74

F

firebox, 17, 35–38, 53
Fogg, Francis S., 66, 76
Fry, James B., 71, 76–77

G

Gailey and Boyd, 63
Gailey, David A., 63, 72, 77

General Harney, 18
Gilbert, J. J., 31, 77
Gillette, E. C., 3, 67, 75, 77–78, 81
Great Depression, 13, 29–30
Gregg, Nathan P., 64, 73, 77-78, 80

H

Hanford, C. H., 23, 55, 78
Hawaii, 12, 14, 41, 45
Henry Cowell Lime and Cement Company, 63
Hibbard, Augustin, 3, 5, 67, 71, 78, 80, 83, 85
Huntington, Charles, 5, 67, 71, 78

I

Ingram, Lee, 9, 78
Island Lime Company, 7, 10, 63, 71, 73–74, 77, 82, 86

J

J. B. Libby, 19
Jamieson, Robert, 10, 61, 72, 78-79
Judd Cove, 50–53, 61, 64, 72–73, 77–79

K

Keen, J. M., 79
Kirkwood, W. W., 79
Kittinger, George B., 64, 79, 80

L

Langdon, 3-4, 10–11, 13, 65–66, 68, 74, 76–77, 79–81, 83–85
Lee, Thomas H., 76, 79
Lime Kiln, 1–3, 6–7, 23, 32–39, 61, 63–64, 71–75, 77–84

M

Manning, L. R., 69, 79–80, 85
Maskey, Thomas, 80
Masterson, Charles P., 80, 85
McCurdy Lime Company, 10, 52–53, 64, 73, 78, 80, 85
McCurdy, Catherine, 5-6, 67, 72, 78, 80
McCurdy, James, 6-7, 10, 52, 67-68, 72, 80
McGraw & Kittinger, 64, 70
McGraw, John H., 64, 79, 80
McLachlan, Daniel, 65, 81
McMillin, John S., 9, 22–24, 41, 46, 48, 67–69, 73, 75, 79–82, 85
McMillin, Louella Hiett, 26, 48
McMillin, Paul, 40, 47-48
Mitchell Bay Lime Company, 63, 65, 74

N

Nagaoka, Shigeru, 81
Newsome, Frank, 3, 67, 75, 77, 81
Nottingham, Charles W., 81-82

O

Orcas Lime Company, 62, 65, 70, 75–76, 83

P

Panic of 1893, 12, 25
paper rock, 13, 30–31, 62, 65, 74
Paxson, T. T., 82
Port Langdon, 3-4, 10–11, 13, 65–66, 68, 74, 76–77, 79–81, 83–85
Port Townsend, 5, 12, 19, 67, 74, 78–82

Portland, Oregon, 12, 24, 69–70, 82, 84
Portland cement, 27–28, 69, 73, 75
Puget Sound Cement & Lime Company, 66, 70, 83
Puget Sound Lime Company, 66, 86
pulp, 13, 30

Q

quarrying, 3, 15, 26, 33, 43, 61, 84
Queen Brick & Lime Company, 66-67
quicklime, 13, 18

R

Roche Harbor, 1, 3, 9, 14, 18–31, 40–49, 57-61, 67–69, 72-75, 77, 81-85
Roche Harbor Lime and Cement Company, 27, 41, 67, 69, 72, 74
Ross, Alexander, Colin, and Donald, 9, 69, 81–82

S

San Juan Archipelago Lime Company, 67
San Juan Lime Company, 3–9, 11, 20, 33–34, 52, 63–64, 67–68, 75, 78, 80, 82–83, 85
Scurr, Richard and Robert, 9, 41, 82
Seattle, 12, 24, 62–71, 73–75, 77–81, 84–86
Seattle & Roche Harbor Lime Company, 68, 83
Shotter & Company, 65, 68, 81-83
Shotter, George R., 4–5, 65, 67, 78, 82-83
Shultz, William, 26, 69, 74, 83
Soderberg, 62–63, 66, 68, 70, 83–85
Soderberg, J. A., 62, 83
Spokane, 24
Standard Lime Company, 65–66, 68, 76, 80, 84

Star of Chile, 45

Staveless Barrell Company, 26, 68, 79

Stuart Island Lime Company, 69

sugar rock, 14

T

T. W. Lake, 19

Tacoma, 12–13, 22–24, 26–28, 61, 66–72, 74–75, 79–83, 85

Tacoma and Roche Harbor Lime Company, 9, 22–24, 26–28, 31, 41, 67–71, 79–81, 83, 85

Tacoma Lime Company, 22–23, 69, 82

Tallentire, Thomas, 68, 83

Tevis, Lloyd, 9, 78, 84

Tift, A. D., 84

Township and Range Survey, 7, 56

Tuck, Ed, 84

Tulloch, James, 15, 84

U

U. S. North West Boundary Survey, 3

W

Wa Chung, 84

Wadhams & Elliott, 70

Wadhams, William, 70, 84-85

Wallace, Thomas B., 85

Walter & Soderburg, 68, 70

Walter, M. H., 61, 70, 72, 85

Watts, Charles, 5, 67, 71-72, 78, 85

Werner, J. C., 62, 71, 85

Westerman Lime & Rock, 64, 70

Wheeler, Lee and L. H., 61, 63, 66, 86
White Point, 70, 75, 82
William G. Irwin, 18, 45
Wing Ha, 86

NOTES

www.ingramcontent.com/pod-product-compliance
Lightning Source LLC
Chambersburg PA
CBHW061730070526
44583CB00024B/3077